Quarto is the authority on a wide range of topics.

Quarto educates, entertains and enriches the lives of our readers—enthusiasts and lovers of hands-on living.

www.QuartoKnows.com

© 2017 Quarto Publishing Group USA Inc.
Original artwork and project designs © 2017 Cassie Stephens

First published in the United States of America in 2017 by
Quarry Books, an imprint of
Quarto Publishing Group USA Inc.
100 Cummings Center, Suite 265-D
Beverly, Massachusetts 01915-6101
Telephone: (978) 282-9590
Fax: (978) 283-2742
QuartoKnows.com
Visit our blogs at QuartoKnows.com

10 9 8 7 6 5 4 3 2 1

ISBN: 978-1-63159-270-6

Digital edition published in 2017.

Library of Congress Cataloging-in-Publication Data available.

Design and Page Layout: Laura H. Couallier, Laura Herrmann Design
Cover Image: Patrick F. Smith Photography
Photography: Patrick F. Smith Photography: pages 6, 8, 18, 42, 78, 90, 114, and 120. All other photography by Cassie Stephens.

Printed in China

DEDICATION

This book is dedicated to all of the bright and budding young artists I've had the privilege to share the joy of mess making with over the past twenty years. Together we have learned, laughed, and grown. Here's to many more messes and masterpieces!

CASSIE STEPHENS

CLAY LAB *for kids*

52 Projects to Make, Model, and
Mold with Air-Dry, Polymer,
and Homemade Clay

QUARRY

CONTENTS

INTRODUCTION

Nearly twenty years ago, I was in college, filling my days with studio art classes and my nights with hours of painting. While it was an absolute dream come true for me, my parents, who were paying for my education, weren't so certain the dream would become a reality. When my parents suggested I also take some art education classes, I was seriously doubtful. What did I know about teaching art to children? Fast-forward to the present: I've been teaching all this time. I still have much to learn, but I know one thing for certain: Kids love to create as much as I do.

If you were to ask the hundreds of children I've taught over the years what their favorite art activity is, they'd respond with an enthusiastic "clay!" There's something about working with your hands, creating something three-dimensional and functional, not to mention getting messy, that really captures every child's heart and imagination. When my students come back to visit, I always hear that they still have that coil mug, clay fish, or snowman sculpture on display in their homes.

In this book, we'll explore the many different clay mediums available that do not require kiln fire. From air-dry and paper clays to polymer and clays you can make with household ingredients, this book introduces 52 clay labs to experience and inspire. Have fun and happy creating!

CREATING WITH KIDS AND CLAY

~~~~~~~~~~

Children are born artists.

They instinctually know how to dig their fingers into clay or to put crayon to paper (or the walls in your home, if you're not careful!) and create something magical. You might not understand the images you see, but when children proudly explain it to you, their imagination is evident.

This book is for children who love to get a little messy, work with their hands, and create memories. All that's to say: This book is for the artist who lives in us all!

HOW THIS BOOK IS ORGANIZED

This book is divided by units of non-fired clays: air-dry, polymer, and homemade. When creating with these various types of clay bodies, young artists will notice the differences between them and may take a liking to one over the other. Some clay is water-based and sticky, while others are not. Despite the differences in ingredients and texture, almost all of the clay used in these labs is interchangeable. Go ahead and explore, using your preferred clay in any lab!

These labs allow kids to explore each medium, learn new techniques, and be inspired. Each creative idea leads to another, picking up momentum like a ball rolling downhill. However, the labs do not have to be completed in the order presented. Allow your young artists to create what piques their interests. One child might want to create a project exactly as it's made in this book. Another might choose to take the idea in a completely new direction. All directions are good ones.

Within many of the labs, there are adaptive suggestions for the developing artist. When younger siblings work alongside an older brother or sister, it can be frustrating for the young ones to match what they perceive as a certain standard. Coax them gently. Teach them that developing strong hand muscles and skill takes time. Introduce them to the adaptive methods suggested. Most of all, relax, create, and have fun together!

BASIC SUPPLIES

Let's talk about the tools and materials you'll need to start your own clay lab. Here is a basic list of what you'll need for your clay adventures:

A COVERED AND CLUTTER-FREE WORKSPACE

I like to work on my dining room table. However, I don't want the clay to stain or damage my table, so I always place a large sheet of clean white paper down before I work. A roll of paper is my preferred table covering because it allows me to simply tear off a sheet, work, and recycle it when finished. Newspaper, a plastic placemat, or a large sheet of cardboard would work as well. Canvas is a good choice, too, because it can be washed and reused.

DROP CLOTH

You'll need this if you're working in a room with carpeting. Dropped pieces of clay ground into the fibers of a carpet can be difficult to remove.

SMOCK OR APRON

The clays used in this book require only soap-and-water cleanup. However, young artists often have the habit of wiping their hands on their clothing. A smock or an apron will keep them a little cleaner.

BABY WIPES

For children who might not like the texture of some of the clays or the sensation of dried clay on their hands, baby wipes are a handy solution.

ROLLING PIN OR LARGE JAR

For these projects, you'll often need to flatten a slab of clay. A rolling pin will do the job, but a large jar works just as well. However, pounding clay flat is my students' favorite option. I tell them to aim for "cookie thickness." Once flat, flip the clay over to the smooth, non-pounded side. Allow your artists to pick their favorite flattening method.

TEXTURED MATERIALS

One of the fun things about clay is that it can capture texture. I use the soles of my shoes, burlap, old sweaters, and even lace to create texture. Save pieces of textured plastic, cardboard, knits, and more for playing with clay.

SKEWERS

Skewers are pointed wooden sticks for making kabobs. They're inexpensive and available at many grocery stores. We use them in our labs for cutting clay and poking holes. We also use them for the slip and score method of joining two pieces of clay.

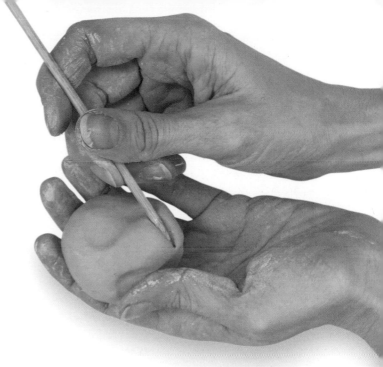

Slip-and-Score

Slip is another word for watery clay and score means to scratch. To join two pieces, score the surfaces of both (a skewer works well), moisten the surfaces with water, and press the two pieces together. In this book, the slip-and-score method is done with toothbrushes and skewers.

OLD TOOTHBRUSH

When working with air-dry clays, toothbrushes work very well for slipping, scoring, and attaching clay pieces. To attach pieces of air-dry clay to one another, gently scrub both pieces of clay with a slightly dampened toothbrush. A toothbrush is also a handy tool for creating texture on clay.

WATER IN A SPILLPROOF CUP

With the exception of polymer clay, all of the clays in this book will need water as you work with them. Water acts as glue for many projects and is also useful for smoothing surface cracks. Keep just a small amount of water available in a shallow bowl to prevent spills. Dog bowls are great alternatives to water cups because they are created to be spillproof. You can find them inexpensively at your local dollar store.

TOOTHPICKS, PAPERCLIPS, PENCILS, AND STICKS

The scratched, poked, and embossed details of many projects in this book were created by using everyday household objects. Keep a creative eye open and put together a box of items that will add to your clay explorations.

GARLIC PRESS

An inexpensive garlic press is a fun tool to keep on hand. When used with air-dry clay, it creates a spaghetti-like texture that can be used for hair, beards, grass, or foliage.

DENTAL FLOSS

Some air-dry clay comes in thick blocks. An easy and effective way to cut clay from a large block is with dental floss. Simply wrap the floss around your index fingers and pull it through the clay to slice off a nice even piece.

BABY OIL

Polymer clay can dry out and become crumbly and hard to work with. If this happens, simply put a few drops of baby oil on your hands and massage it into the clay. As you work, the clay will return to its soft, pliable state.

SOAP, WATER, AND A GENTLE BRUSH

Some of the darker shades of polymer clay can temporarily stain hands. Use warm soapy water and a gentle brush to easily remove the coloring.

DULL BUTTER KNIFE

This is the perfect tool for cutting clay cleanly, with no danger to small hands.

VARIETIES OF CLAY

The wide variety of clays to choose from can be overwhelming. The key is to allow your child to try several types. Each has its own texture and feel, qualities, and curing method. Exploring many options allows your artist to discover his or her favorites.

POLYMER CLAY

Polymer clays are widely available in a tempting variety of colors. But you don't have to purchase every polymer color to make your creations. In our Polymer Unit, we'll show you how to create your own colors as well as exploring the medium to its fullest!

Polymer clay is hardened by baking it in an ordinary kitchen oven or toaster oven. Directions vary by manufacturer, and the baking must be done with adult supervision. Overbaking can cause fumes. Be sure to allow polymer projects to cool thoroughly before handling.

Polymer clay is nontoxic, but all the same, take certain precautions with it. Kids should wash their hands after using it, and they should not try to taste it. Tools that are used for preparing food should not be used with the clay, and polymer crafts should not be used for serving food.

Store leftover polymer clay in a glass container. Alternatively, you can sort the clay by color in a paper egg carton. Don't use plastic containers or plastic wrap because they can cause a reaction with polymer clay.

AIR-DRY CLAY

Craft stores sell many varieties of air-dry clay. Each has a unique set of properties, but you don't need to purchase them all! Buy one at a time and explore each to its fullest to decide which you like best. Many of the labs lend themselves to several types of clay, not just the one suggested.

The down side to air-dry clay is that it takes a long time to dry, which can be difficult for impatient young artists. To expedite the drying process, set the clay in the sun on a warm day. While drying, be certain to turn the clay over and allow the back side to dry as well. If the clay is not rotated, mold can grow on the damp underside. When you're finished working with air-dry clay, wrap it tightly with plastic wrap and store it in a sealed bag. This will prevent the clay from drying out.

POLYFORM MODEL AIR/ AIR-DRY MODELING CLAY

This clay comes in both white and terra cotta. When it dries, it looks much like kiln-fired clay, but projects made from this clay may take up to a week to dry. It must be kept in an airtight zipper-lock bag when not in use.

PLUS MODELING CLAY

This clay looks and feels like kiln-fired clay. It's sticky and messy, just like the real thing! Like the Polyform clay, it's water-based and should be kept in an airtight bag. Again, allow for several days of drying time and don't forget to rotate to avoid mold.

CREATIVE PAPERCLAY MODELING MATERIAL

This clay is very lightweight and fun to work with. It's prone to drying out as you work, so keep water on hand to smooth out cracks. Be sure to store it in an airtight zipper-lock bag.

HOMEMADE CLAY

What do you do when you don't have store-bought clay available to work with? You make your own, of course! In fact, a lot of the fun of homemade clay is making it. You will find that each recipe has its special crafting properties. You might enjoy some more than others, but one thing is for certain, you'll have a good time with it! Almost all of the home-made clay recipes are no-cook and no-bake. When baking is called for, be certain an adult supervises.

Each type of homemade clay has its own recipe. Read over each recipe carefully to be sure you have all of the necessary items. You'll also need a mixing bowl, measuring cups and spoons, an apron, and a clean work surface.

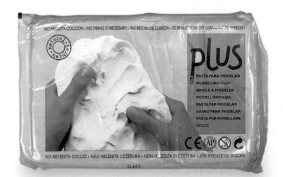

OTHER SUPPLIES

WATERCOLOR, ACRYLIC, OR GOUACHE PAINTS

Just like clay, different paints have different qualities. For the beginner artist, watercolor is a wonderful choice because it is easy to use, mix into new colors, and clean up. Watercolor is translucent, which does not lend itself to complete coverage when painting. For that, acrylic paint works well. Small bottles of acrylic paint in a variety of colors are available at craft stores. However, acrylic doesn't always wash off textiles and other surfaces, so keep that in mind. Gouache is a versatile paint that offers the best of both worlds: it can be translucent or opaque depending on how it is applied. It is also washable.

Once you finish creating with air-dry or homemade clays, you might want to add color. Watercolors work nicely if you want the color of the clay to show through. Gouache is more opaque and allows you to blend colors as you would with watercolor. Acrylic is great for complete color coverage.

MOD PODGE OR CLEAR SEALER

To seal and protect finished pieces, brush on a matte or gloss sealer. When you're working with children, use a nontoxic, acrylic-based sealant such as Mod Podge. Acrylic-based sealants are fume free, they dry quickly, and they wash up with soap and water. Best of all, they are safe for children to use, too. But acrylic-based sealants are not water- and weather-proof, so make sure your young artists don't leave their finished projects outdoors.

TIPS FOR WORKING WITH KIDS AND CLAY

There is always a learning curve when trying something new. This can cause frustration for young artists and lead to a chorus of "I can'ts." To prevent that from happening, chat with the children before each session. Let them know that they will be learning something new, which takes time and patience. Have a "no-negative-talk" rule during creativity time. A small change in vocabulary from "I can't" to "I can if I keep trying" makes a world of a difference.

When working with a group of children, teach them the buddy system. If they see a buddy who is struggling, allow them to reteach the instructions. I have found that children are often better at explaining directions to each other than I am because they speak the same language.

Don't do the work for the children. If you decide to create alongside of children, never pick up their pieces and work on them. This indicates that you are the artist and they aren't. Simply get a new piece of clay and go over the steps slowly with them on your own piece. They will be happier with a finished work of art that they created themselves.

Try to save your child's works of art, even if just temporarily. Not everything your child creates will be a masterpiece. However, even the lesser pieces are important in showing growth. Jot down the date the work was created. Later, gather up the projects and arrange them chronologically. Your little artist will be motivated to continue creating.

Air-dry and homemade clay can become fragile once dry if it is rolled or pinched too thin. I like to use the measurement "as thick as a cookie" for rolling or pounding clay flat. This rule does not apply to polymer clay.

A little goes a long way when working with clay. Instead of allowing your child to work with an entire package of air-dry or polymer clay, cut off a small portion for use and add more as needed.

In my art room, my students work on a surface covered in paper with a plastic placemat on top. They use a damp soapy sponge to wipe down their placemats. After several days, the paper is recycled and replaced. This keeps tables clean and cleanup a snap.

Have a small broom and dust pan available for your child to sweep up any clay that may have fallen to the floor. A small handheld vacuum would work well for carpeted rooms.

CLEANUP AND CARING FOR YOUR SUPPLIES

Working with clay and managing the mess is the art of controlled chaos. Cover the work surface, the floor if necessary, and your young artist. Take heart in knowing that these clays clean up with soap and water. Most of the fun is in the mess-making!

I'm a firm believer in having a dedicated space to create in. Even if it's a small desk, a corner of the dining table, or a TV tray, having a space available with the basic supplies, a variety of clays, and this book neatly stored will inspire kids to create.

Teaching good cleanup techniques will ensure that supplies have a long art-making life. Skewers, rolling pins, brushes, and palettes should be washed thoroughly. If time is an issue, have a plastic tub with warm soapy water available to allow tools to soak.

AIR-DRY CLAYS AND LEARNING THE BASICS

A wide variety of air-dry clays

are available. It's fun to explore their different properties with the labs in this chapter. Some of your young artists will prefer one variety over others, so keep in mind that you can use any air-dry clay in any of the following labs.

Air-dry clay is water-based, so keep a spillproof cup of water on the work table in case the clay becomes dry and difficult to manipulate. Drying time varies for different brands of air-dry clay and for different thicknesses. Rotate finished projects as they dry to ensure even and thorough drying.

SHOE-STAMPED POTTERY

One of the coolest things about clay is its ability to capture textures. In this lab, you'll experiment with creating textures in clay by using the indentations on the soles of shoes. Use as many shoes as you can find to create a variety of textures to decorate the rim of this unique piece of pottery. But beware: The dirt stuck in the bottoms of shoes will end up stuck in your clay, so use shoes with clean soles.

Tools & Materials

air-dry clay
(I used paper clay
for this lab.)

shoes

terra cotta pot

water

paintbrushes

acrylic paint

metallic acrylic paint

1 Begin by rolling several balls of clay in your hands. To roll a ball of clay, place it between your hands. Gently add pressure as you rotate your hands in circles. (Fig. 1)

2 Find shoes with clean soles that have a variety of patterns and textures. Firmly press each ball of clay into the indentations in the soles. Flatten each piece slightly and then peel it off. You'll see the texture in the clay. (Fig. 2 & 3)

3 Set out the terra cotta pot. Moisten the back of one of the pieces of clay with a little water and press it gently onto the rim of the pot. Continue until the rim is covered with overlapping stamped pieces. (Fig. 4)

4 Allow the pot to dry for several days. Paint the stamped pieces along the rim with acrylic paint. Once it's dry, gently paint over the color with a metallic acrylic paint to give it a bit of shine and show off the shoe-stamped texture. (Fig. 5)

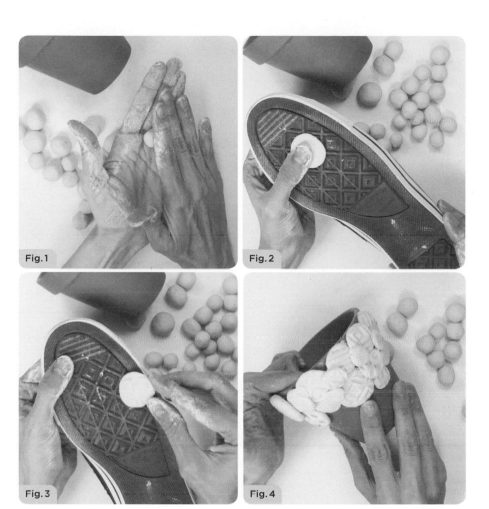

Fig. 1

Fig. 2

Fig. 3

Fig. 4

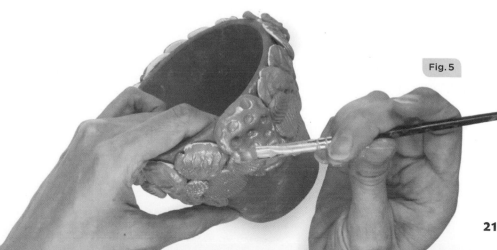

Fig. 5

COFFEE AND A DONUT

In this lab, you'll learn many of the basics for sculpting with clay: how to create a pinch pot, a slab or a flattened piece of clay, and a coil or rolled piece of clay. You'll put all of these new skills together to create a coffee cup, saucer, and donut!

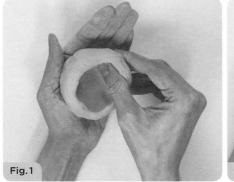

Fig. 1

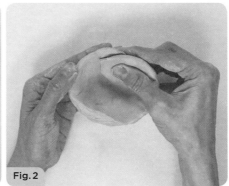

Fig. 2

1 Begin by placing a ball of clay the size of a small orange in the palm of your hand. With your other hand, place your thumb on top and your fingers around the back. Push your thumb firmly into the clay until it gets close to the bottom but does not go all the way through. (Fig. 1)

2 Remove your thumb from the clay. The opening you've created is the start of a pinch pot. To make the pot bigger, put your thumb back into the opening and use your fingers to pinch the sides. Turn the pot as you pinch until the sides and the bottom are the thickness of a cookie.

Tools & Materials

white water-based air-dry clay (I used Amaco Marblex.)

water

toothbrush

crayons

watercolor paint

paintbrushes

puffy paint

Mod Podge

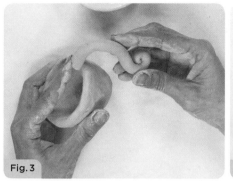
Fig. 3

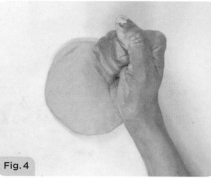
Fig. 4

Fig. 5

3 If the pinch pot loses its shape, make a 1" (2.5 cm) tear in the clay. Overlap the two torn edges and smooth the seam with your fingers. Repeat on the opposite side of the pot. (Fig. 2)

4 To make the handle for the cup, pinch off a piece of clay the size of a gumball. Roll it up and down in your hands to make a snake of clay. The snake should be as thick as your finger and even all the way across.

5 Roll one end of the snake to make a coil. Bend the snake into a handle shape and hold it up to your pinch pot. Trim the snake if necessary and attach it: Scratch the pinch pot with a wet tooth-brush where you want the handle to go. Push the handle onto the scratched spot and smooth it until it sticks. Set the cup aside. (Fig. 3)

6 To create the plate for the donut, start with a piece of clay the size of a small orange. Roll it into a ball. Place it on your work surface and pound it flat. Stop pounding the clay when it's as thick as a cookie and level all the way across. Set it aside. (Fig. 4)

7 For the donut, start with a golf ball–sized piece of clay. Roll it up and down in your hands. Stop when it is 6" (15 cm) long. Bend it to make the letter *O*. To connect the ends for the *O*, rub both with a wet toothbrush, overlap, and smooth together. Set aside all three clay pieces to dry for about a week. (Fig. 5)

8 Use crayons to draw designs and watercolors to add designs to the cup and plate and paint the donut. To make the donut look more realistic, add sprinkles or icing with puffy paint. Allow the paint to dry.

9 To seal and protect your treasures, add a coat of Mod Podge. (Fig. 6)

Fig. 6

TEXTURED LANDSCAPE PLAQUE

In this lab, you'll learn the skills to create a landscape of your choice, such as an underwater scene, a sunset on a beach, or a mountainous view—use your imagination! Hang your creation on the wall or show it off on a small easel.

Tools & Materials

air-dry clay
(I used Amaco
Marblex.)

skewer

textured fabric

rolling pin or jar

toothbrush

water

garlic press

watercolor paint
or gouache

paintbrushes

Mod Podge

1 Start with a piece of clay the size of an orange. Roll or pound the clay into a flat slab that is even and as thick as a cookie. If you like, use the skewer to trim the edges into a shape, such as a rectangle or circle, or leave it rough. (Fig. 1)

2 Tear off a fresh piece of clay the size of a golf ball. Pound it flat onto the fabric. This piece can be paper thin. (Fig. 2)

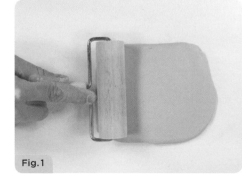

Fig.1

Fig.2

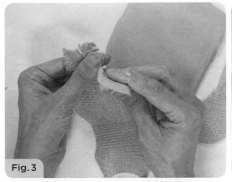

Fig. 3

Fig. 4

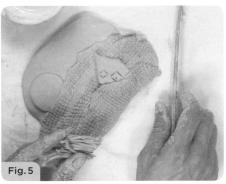

Fig. 5

Fig. 6

5 Think about adding a sun, moon, stars, or clouds to the sky. Pound the clay flat and use a skewer to cut out these shapes. Use the toothbrush to attach them to the slab.

6 Place a small ball of clay in the back of the garlic press and squeeze to create grass. Attach it to the slab with a moistened toothbrush. (Fig. 5)

7 Consider adding a house, a family pet, or trees to the landscape. Again, cut those out of flattened clay, scrub the backs gently with a wet toothbrush, and attach. (Fig. 6)

8 If the plaque is to be hung, poke two holes at the top with the skewer. Allow it to dry for up to a week and then feed a string through the holes.

9 Paint the plaque with water-color or gouache. Allow the paint to dry.

10 Seal and protect your plaque with Mod Podge. (Fig. 7)

3 Tear the textured clay in half lengthwise. This will be the "land" for your landscape. Gently place it on the first slab to see how it looks and then remove. Create hills and landscape features with different textures. (Fig. 3)

4 Attach the landscape pieces to the slab by scratching the surfaces with a wet toothbrush and pressing them gently into place. (Fig. 4)

Fig. 7

CUPCAKE CONTAINERS

Who says your clay projects can't look good enough to eat? These fun cupcakes aren't just for decoration. They're also containers that can hold your tiniest treasures. In this lab, you'll use the pinch pot and coil-making skills you have learned. Any air-dry clay would work well here.

Tools & Materials

air-dry clay
(I used ACTIVA Plus
Clay Natural
Self-Hardening White.)

skewer

water

toothbrush

acrylic paint
in several colors

paintbrushes

Mod Podge

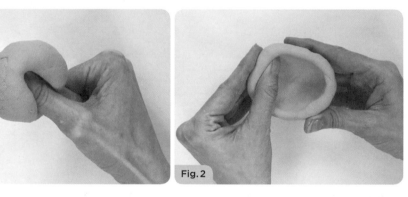

Fig. 1

Fig. 2

1 Pinch off a piece of clay about the size of a golf ball. Roll it into a ball.

2 Place the ball in the palm of one hand. Press the thumb of your other hand firmly into the center of the ball. Be certain not to go all the way through the clay with your thumb. (Fig. 1)

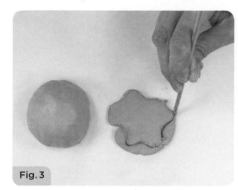

Fig. 3

Fig. 4

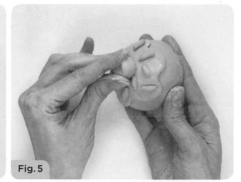

Fig. 5

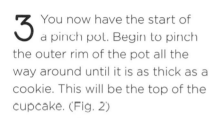

Fig. 6

Fig. 7

3 You now have the start of a pinch pot. Begin to pinch the outer rim of the pot all the way around until it is as thick as a cookie. This will be the top of the cupcake. (Fig. 2)

4 Set the cupcake top on your work surface like a dome and get ready to decorate it. To create icing, flatten a piece of clay the size of a gumball between your fingers. Place it on the table. Use a skewer to carve icing shapes using a wavy line. Scrub the top of the pinch pot with a wet toothbrush and add the icing. (Fig. 3 & 4)

5 Create sprinkles by rolling small pieces of clay. Use the wet toothbrush to attach the sprinkles in place. Roll a small ball of clay to add to the top for a cherry. (Fig. 5)

6 For swirled icing, roll a long snake of clay. Roll it into a coil by bending it around itself. Attach the start of the coil to the top of the pinch pot. Then wrap the rest of the snake around the pinch pot. (Fig. 6)

7 To create the bottom of the cupcake, create a smaller pinch pot, so that the top of the cupcake fits over it. (If the bottom is too wide, follow step 3 in Lab 2, page 23, to make it narrower.)

Press this pinch pot firmly onto the surface of a table so that it stands without toppling over. Using a skewer, draw lines to show the texture of a cupcake liner. (Fig. 7)

8 Allow the top and bottom of the cupcake to dry separately for several days.

9 Use acrylic paint to decorate the cupcake and all of the decorations. Allow the paint to dry. Seal the cupcake with Mod Podge.

STACK OF PANCAKES

A tall stack of pancakes is a delicious treat. With air-dry clay, you can serve up a stack as tall as you like with as much syrup, butter, and fruit as you desire. The best part is, this flap-jack stack also serves as a fun container to hold your treasures! This pot is made by stacking coils around the edge of a circular base.

Tools & Materials

air-dry clay
(I used DAS air-dry
modeling clay.)

toothbrush

water

skewer

paint in golden brown
and other colors

paintbrushes

Mod Podge

Fig. 1

Fig. 2

1 Begin by pinching off a piece of clay about the size of a baseball. Flatten the clay by first squeezing it between your hands and then pounding it flat. It should be the size, shape, and thickness of an actual pancake. (Fig. 1)

2 This will be the base of the pancake pot. To make the stack, pinch off a fresh piece of clay the size of a gumball and roll it into a ball. Roll it between your hands to make it longer. Place it on your work surface and roll it from the middle out to the ends to make a snake of clay. It should be about as thick as a finger. (Fig. 2)

Fig. 3

Fig. 4

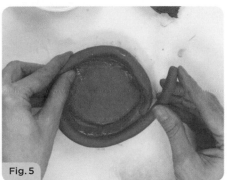

Fig. 5

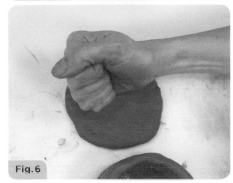

Fig. 6

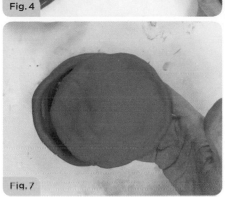

Fig. 7

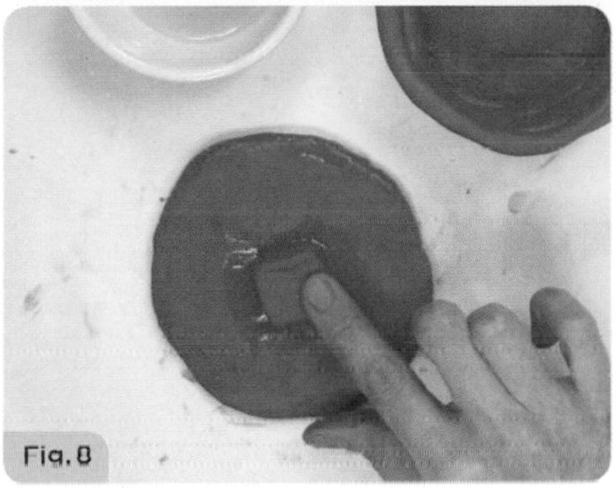

Fig. 8

3 Start adding the sides to your pancake pot. Use the toothbrush and water to gently scrub around the outer edge of the base and along one side of the snake. Coil the snake around the edge of the base, pressing the wet, scrubbed surfaces together. (Fig. 3 & 4)

4 If the clay snake cracks, gently rub water into the cracks. If it breaks apart, overlap the two ends and roll them back together.

5 Continue rolling out more snakes and adding them to the pancake pot until it is at the height you want. (Fig. 5)

6 To make the lid, repeat step 1. It should be slightly wider than the pot. (Fig. 6 & 7)

7 Use the skewer to cut out a small square piece of clay. Attach it to the lid. Use your extra clay to create fruit by molding the shapes in your hand. Attach them to the side of the stack of pancakes. (Fig. 8)

8 Dry the lid on a flat surface, not the top of the stack of pancake. Allow the pot to dry for up to a week before painting.

9 Paint the pancakes golden brown and allow the paint to dry. Seal the pancakes with Mod Podge.

COIL PRESS POT

This lab teaches you how to make a pot by pressing it into a mold. Many objects around your home can be used as molds. Unless they are terra cotta, they will need to be lined in plastic wrap so the clay does not stick. Press the clay on the inside of the mold, not the outside, because clay shrinks as it dries. The type of coils you created in Lab 5 will be used again here. This time, you'll learn to bend and shape the coils to create interesting designs!

Tools & Materials

small, wide mouthed bowl

plastic wrap

air-dry clay
(I used ACTIVA Plus
Clay Natural
Self-Hardening White.)

water

acrylic paint

paintbrushes

Mod Podge

1 Cover the interior of the bowl in plastic wrap to prevent the clay from sticking.

2 Pinch off a Ping-Pong ball–size piece of clay and roll it into a ball. Roll the clay up and down between your hands until it resembles a hot dog, Place it on your work surface and roll it with your fingers to stretch and lengthen it like a snake. Start in the middle and work your hands out to the ends. The snake should be as thick as a thumb. (Fig. 1)

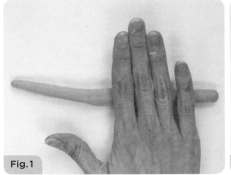

Fig.1

Fig.2

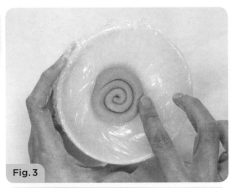

Fig.3

Fig.4

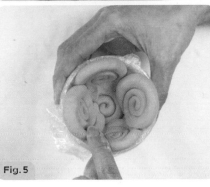

Fig.5

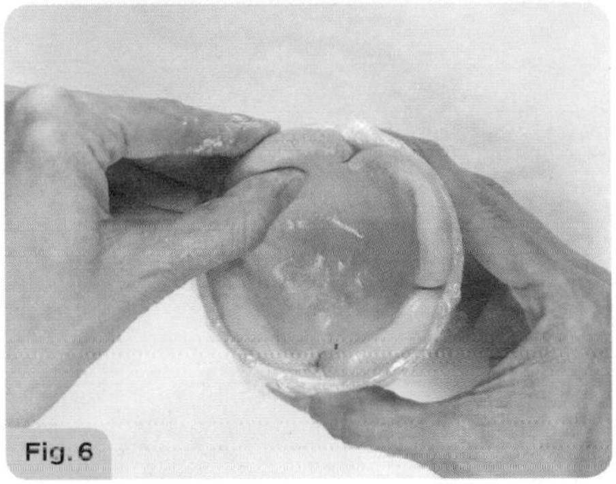

Fig.6

3 Stop and check the snake every now and then. It should be the same thickness all the way across. If it breaks, don't worry about it! Just overlap the two ends and resume rolling.

4 Begin coiling the snake into a spiral, using your work surface for support. Start with the center of the coil, bending the snake into a tight *C* shape, and then round and round, with the spiral layers pressed together. (Fig. 2)

5 Press the coil into the bottom of the bowl. (Fig. 3)

6 Follow steps 2 through 4 to create four more coils. Add them, one at a time, to the inside of the bowl, beginning where the previous coil ended and continuing up the sides of the bowl. (Fig. 4)

7 Press the coils in place inside the bowl. Fill in any gaps with small pieces of clay. (Fig. 5)

8 With a wet finger, smooth the clay inside the bowl. (Fig. 6)

9 Set it aside to allow the clay to dry for several days. Gently remove the bowl from the mold.

10 Paint the bowl with a variety of colors and allow them to dry. Seal the bowl with Mod Podge.

MONOGRAM WALL HANGING

In Lab 1, you pressed clay into the soles of your shoes for a fun texture. Let's find out what happens when you press clay into textured fabric. This will provide a background for a wall hanging featuring your initials. I used burlap, lace, and doilies to create mine.

Tools & Materials

textured fabric

air-dry clay
(I used Crayola
Air-Dry Clay.)

rolling pin or jar

large cookie cutters

toothbrush

skewer

water

paint
(I used fluorescent
tempera cakes.)

paintbrushes

Mod Podge

string or ribbon

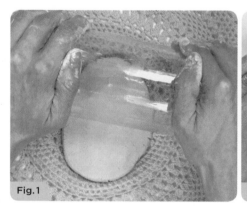

Fig. 1

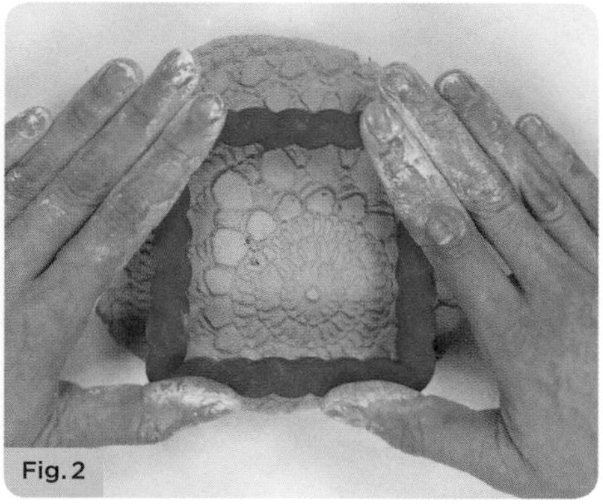

Fig. 2

1 Place the textured fabric on your work surface. Pinch off a piece of clay the size of a small orange. Stand up to press the clay firmly into the fabric. Roll or pound the clay to flatten it. Stop when the clay is as thick and level as a cookie. (Fig. 1)

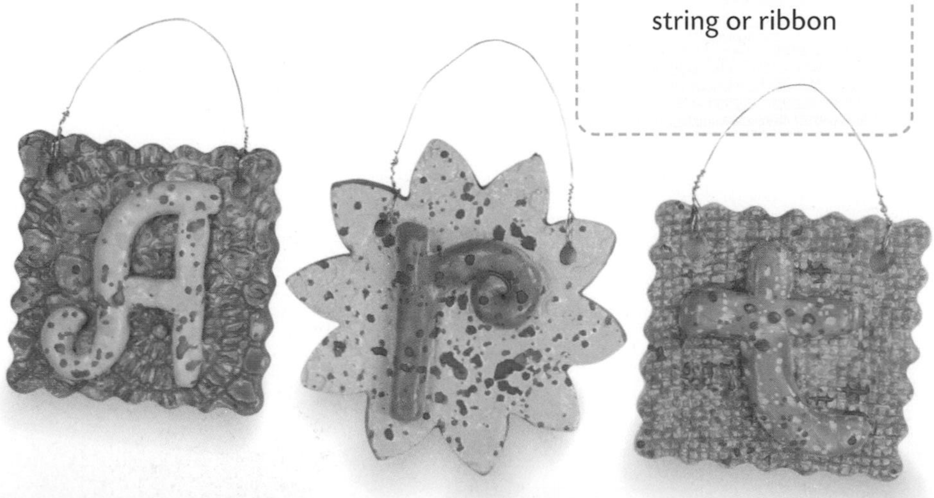

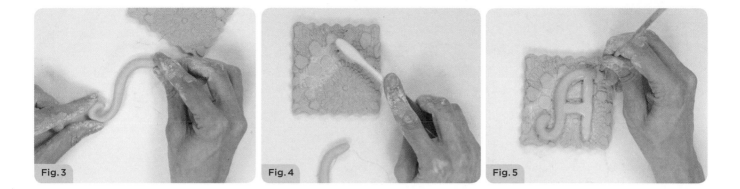

Fig. 3

Fig. 4

Fig. 5

2 Gently peel the clay off of the fabric and place it textured-side up on your work surface. Select a cookie cutter and press it through the clay. (Fig. 2)

3 Gather the extra clay and roll it into a ball between your hands. Then roll it on your work surface until it forms a skinny snake.

4 Shape the snake into the first letter of your name. Place it on the piece of clay cut with the cookie cutter. If it doesn't fit, roll it into a ball and try again. If it's difficult making the letter, draw it on a piece of paper. Then follow the shape of the letter with the clay. (Fig. 3)

5 To make the letter stick, use a wet toothbrush to gently scratch the surface of the cookie shape. Firmly press the letter onto the scratched surface. (Fig. 4)

6 Use the skewer to poke two holes at the top of the cookie shape. (Fig. 5)

7 Allow the wall hanging to dry for about a week. When dry, paint the letter. For a fun finish, water down the paint. Dip a large brush into the watery paint and gently tap the back of the brush over the wall hanging for a splattered paint look. (Fig. 6)

8 Once the paint is dry, seal and coat the wall hanging with Mod Podge.

9 Thread the string or ribbon through the holes of your wall hanging. Hang it up and enjoy it!

Fig 6

DROPPED CONE SCULPTURE

What's the worst thing that can happen when you get a cone of your favorite ice cream? You drop it, of course! This fun sculpture is a take on that idea, but it's also a functional container that can hold and hide small items. It's truly a sweet treat to sculpt.

1 Pinch off a piece of clay the size of a small orange and roll it into a ball.

2 Lay out a piece of burlap or another fabric with texture. Place the ball of clay onto the fabric and smash it flat.

3 Flatten it further by rolling the rolling pin or jar in one direction. Turn the piece of fabric and flatten the clay again, rolling in the opposite direction. Stop when the clay is as thick as a cookie. (Fig. 1)

Tools & Materials

air-dry clay
burlap or textured fabric
rolling pin or jar
water
toothbrush
skewer
acrylic paint
paintbrushes
Mod Podge

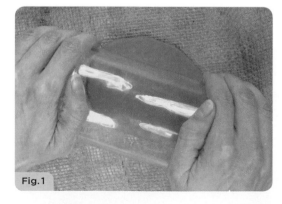

Fig. 1

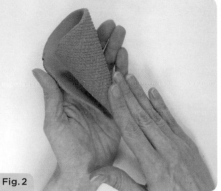

Fig. 2

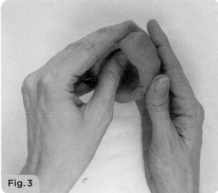

Fig. 3

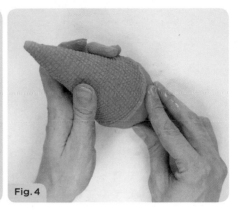

Fig. 4

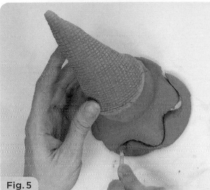

Fig. 5

4 Carefully remove the clay from the fabric.

5 Bend the clay into a cone shape, pointed at one end and wide at the other. Using water and a toothbrush, slip and score the seam. (Fig. 2)

6 Turn the cone point-side up to make sure it can stand on the work surface. Set the cone aside.

7 To make the ice cream, follow steps 1 through 3 in Lab 2 (pages 22–23) for making a pinch pot. (Fig. 3)

8 Turn the pinch pot upside down. Scrub the top with a wet toothbrush. Attach the cone to the open side of the pinch pot. (Fig. 4)

9 To create the splat of ice cream and toppings, use a piece of clay the size of a Ping-Pong ball. Flatten it with your hands and then use the rolling pin to flatten it further.

10 Place the upside down ice cream cone on top. Using a skewer, cut a wavy line through the flattened piece of clay so that it resembles a splat. (Fig. 5)

11 Using scraps of leftover clay, add details such as sprinkles and a cherry to the splat.

12 Once complete, allow it to dry for several days. Dry the splat and the ice cream cone separately so they do not stick together.

13 When the pieces are dry, paint them with a variety of colors. Allow the paint to dry.

14 Seal and protect your dropped cone sculpture with Mod Podge. Hide treasures underneath the upturned ice cream cone!

WAX RESIST LEAF DISH

In this lab, you'll create a shallow dish out of air-dry clay leaves. You'll use real leaves as guides for cutting out the shapes. You'll also press them into the clay to capture the texture of the leaves' veins. The special clay technique you'll experiment with is called *wax resist.* You can use any air-dry clay for this project, though terracotta clay adds a nice fall color to the leaves.

Tools & Materials

air-dry clay

leaves, real or artificial

rolling pin or jar

skewer

shallow dish

plastic wrap

water

crayons

watercolor paint

paintbrushes

Mod Podge

1 Pinch off a Ping-Pong ball–size piece of clay. Roll the clay into a snake, about 3" (7.5 cm) long. Flatten it between your hands.

2 Place a leaf on the table with the vein-side up. Lay the flattened clay on top of the leaf and press it firmly. Roll the clay flat with the rolling pin or jar. The rolled clay should be as thick as a cookie so that it does not become fragile when it dries. (Fig. 1)

3 Turn the clay over—leaf-side up. Using the skewer, cut around the edge of the leaf, all the way through the clay. Holding the stem, gently peel the leaf off of the clay to reveal the texture of the veins. Repeat steps 1 through 3 to create three leaves. (Fig. 2)

Hint: For the best cutting results, keep the skewer vertical and make sure it cuts all of the way through to the work surface.

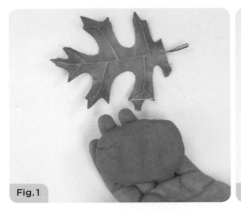

Fig. 1

Fig. 2

Fig. 3

4 Cover the shallow dish with plastic wrap. (This will be the mold for your project. The plastic wrap will prevent the clay leaves from sticking to the dish.) Begin laying the clay leaves onto the dish using the slip and score technique. (Fig. 3)

5 Firmly press the leaves onto the plastic-covered dish.

6 Allow the leaves to dry completely for a couple of days. When the clay is no longer cool to the touch and is lighter in color, it is dry.

7 Remove the clay from the dish.

8 Color the leaves with crayons, and then paint them with watercolors. The wax of the crayons will resist the watercolor paint, which is where *wax resist* gets its name. (Fig. 4 & 5)

9 To seal and protect the piece, coat it in Mod Podge when the paint is dry.

Fig. 4

Fig. 5

LINE RELIEF PENCIL CUP

You've been using many textures in your clay labs. For this pencil holder, you'll create your own raised design. A raised design in a work of art is called a "relief." You'll need a Styrofoam tray for this project. If you use one that once held meat or other food, wash it in hot, soapy water first.

Tools & Materials

ink pen

Styrofoam tray

butter knife

air-dry clay

rolling pin or jar

cornstarch (if needed)

ruler

skewer

water

toothbrush (optional)

watercolor paint or metallic acrylic paints

paintbrushes

clear varnish

varnish brush

1 My favorite part of this project is coming up with the design. Here, I drew several different lines. These lines created shapes, filled with patterns.

2 Use the pen to draw a design on the Styrofoam tray. Go over the lines at least twice. Press down on the pen to make sure the lines are indented, but not cut through, the Styrofoam. (Fig. 1)

3 Use the butter knife to cut off a 2" (5 cm) slab of clay. Press the clay firmly onto the plate design.

4 Roll the clay to cookie thickness with the rolling pin. After rolling the length of the plate, turn the plate and roll the clay in the other direction to cover the entire plate with clay. (Fig. 2)

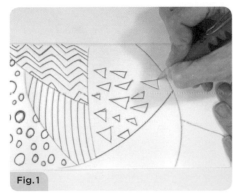
Fig. 1

Fig. 2

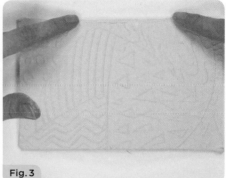
Fig. 3

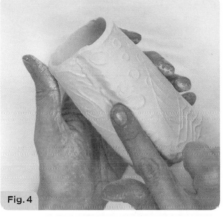
Fig. 4

Fig. 5

5 Slowly peel the clay from the plate. The clay may stick a little because it's moist. If this happens, remove the clay, wash the plate, and try again. This time, sprinkle cornstarch on the surface of the plate to prevent sticking.

6 Using the ruler and a skewer, cut the clay into a rectangle. Dampen your fingers and smooth the rough edges. (Fig. 3)

7 Slip and score one edge of the rectangle with a tooth-brush or skewer. (See page 11 for the slip-and-score technique.) Gently roll the clay into a cylinder shape and join the two short ends of the rectangle. Smooth the edge of the clay. (Fig. 4)

8 To create the base for the pencil holder, use a piece of clay the size of a golf ball. Flatten the clay until it is the same size

as the bottom of the cylinder. Slip and score the edge of the base and connect it to the cylinder. (Fig. 5)

9 Allow the cup to dry for several days.

10 Use watercolor paint or metallic acrylic paint to decorate it. Allow the paint to dry. Seal and protect the piece with clear varnish. (Fig. 6)

Fig. 6

HAMBURGER HOLDER

This hamburger is delicious to look at, but hidden inside are two secret compartments. Keep tiny treasures under the hamburger buns. In this lab, you'll use your knowledge of pinch pot, slab, and coil construction. Just be careful that no one accidently tries to eat your sculpted treat!

Tools & Materials

air-dry clay
(I used Crayola Air
Dry Clay.)

skewer

toothbrush

water

gouache or
watercolor paint

paintbrushes

Mod Podge

Fig. 1

1 Pinch off a piece of clay the size of a small orange. Roll it into a ball and shape it into a pinch pot. This will be the bottom bun of the hamburger. (Fig. 1)

2 To make the pot as shallow as a bun, turn it over and gently tap it on the surface of the table.

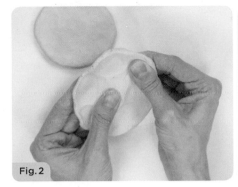

Fig. 2

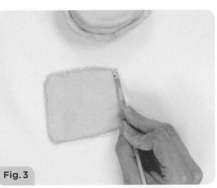

Fig. 3

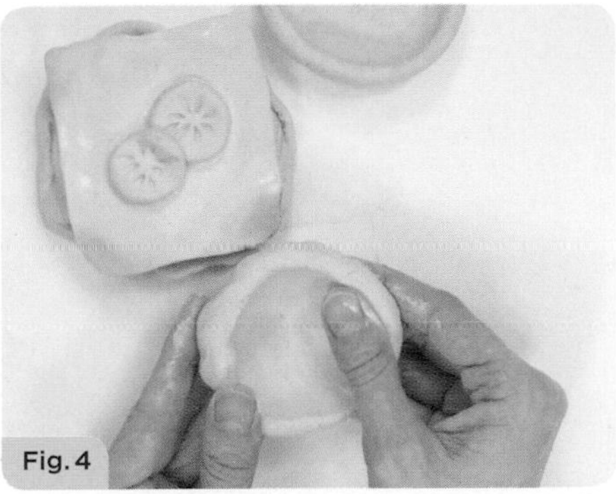

Fig. 4

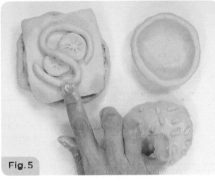

Fig. 5

Fig. 6

3 Pinch off Ping-Pong ball–size pieces of clay for the burger, cheese, tomato slice, and lettuce. Roll these pieces of clay into balls and flatten them onto the work surface. (Fig. 2)

4 I or the hamburger, keep the clay thick. For the lettuce, pound it thin and pinch the edges to give it a wrinkled look. Use the skewer to cut the piece of cheese into a square. (Fig. 3)

5 Rub the top surface of the lettuce and the bottom surface of the burger with the toothbrush and a little water. Press them together. Do the same with the top surface of the burger and the bottom surface of the tomato. Repeat with the top surface of the tomato and the bottom surface of the cheese.

6 Create pickles with small rounds of clay and attach them onto the cheese.

7 To create the top bun, repeat steps 1 and 2. Attach tiny bits of clay to the top of the bun for the sesame seeds. (Fig. 4)

8 Roll a skinny snake of clay for a squirt of ketchup. Attach it to the top of the cheese, as in step 6. (Fig. 5)

9 Allow the two buns and the burger stack to dry separately for up to a week.

10 Paint the burger and buns with gouache or water-color paints. Allow the paint to dry. Seal and protect the pieces with Mod Podge. (Fig. 6)

CLAY SCULPTURE

You have now learned to create

a ball of clay, a rolled and coiled snake of clay, and a slab or flattened piece of clay. You also know to attach clay pieces with the slip-and-score method, which is simply brushing the clay with a wet toothbrush or skewer. In the following labs, you'll see that you can create anything you can dream up with a ball, coil, and slab. Take your knowledge a bit further by exploring the variety of textures you can add to your clay creations.

CLAY COAT OF ARMS

A coat of arms is a personal logo, made up of symbols that represent the person. During the Middle Ages, knights decorated their shields with their coats of arms. That way, even if a knight was covered up with armor on a battlefield, he could be identified by his coat of arms. Think about what special things you would choose to symbolize your unique personality. Then make the symbols out of clay for your very own coat of arms!

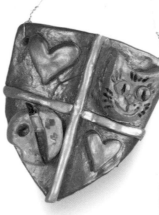

Tools & Materials

dental floss

air-dry clay
(I used Amaco
Marblex.)

skewer

toothbrush

water

crumpled newspaper

metallic acrylic paints

paintbrushes

Mod Podge

1 Cut a 12" (30.5 cm)-long piece of dental floss and pull it tight between your hands. Use it to cut a toast-thick slice from the brick of clay. (Fig. 1)

2 Pound the clay until it is as thick and level as a cookie. Turn the clay over to the smooth side.

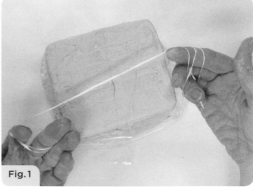

Fig. 1

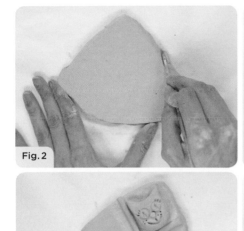
Fig. 2

Fig. 3

Fig. 4

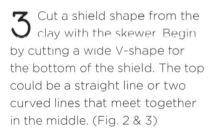
Fig. 5

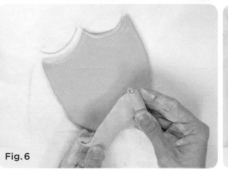
Fig. 6

Fig. 7

3 Cut a shield shape from the clay with the skewer. Begin by cutting a wide V-shape for the bottom of the shield. The top could be a straight line or two curved lines that meet together in the middle. (Fig. 2 & 3)

4 Pinch two small pieces from the brick of clay. Roll each into a skinny snake. Use these strips to divide the shield into four sections. Use the toothbrush to attach the clay strips in place. (Fig. 4)

5 Now it's time to add special symbols. To create shapes such as stars and hearts, pound a piece of clay flat, turn it smooth-side up, and cut out the shapes with the skewer. Attach the shapes to the shield. (Fig. 5)

6 To create animals, visit Lab 21 on page 68. Make letters as shown in Lab 7 on page 32.

7 For a scroll, pound a long, thin rectangle of clay. Roll the ends of the rectangle inward, like a scroll. Attach the scroll to the shield. Write words on the scroll with the skewer. (Fig. 6)

8 Crumple a piece of newspaper and drape the shield over it. This will give it a three-dimensional shape as it dries.

9 If you are going to hang the shield, use the skewer to poke two holes near the top. Allow the shield to dry for a week or more.

10 To give the shield the look of metal, paint it with metallic acrylics. Paint the background first and then paint the details. Allow the paint to dry. Seal and protect it with a coat of Mod Podge. (Fig. 7)

LAB 13 PIE SAFE

Trompe l'oeil is French for "fool the eye." In art, that means an artist has created something so realistic that you are fooled into thinking it's real. Try your hand at this by creating a fun pie safe: a wedge-shaped lidded box that looks just like a slice of pizza, pie, or cake!

Tools & Materials

air-dry clay
(I used Crayola Air
Dry Clay.)

rolling pin or jar

skewer

toothbrush

water

garlic press

gouache or acrylic paint

paintbrushes

Mod Podge

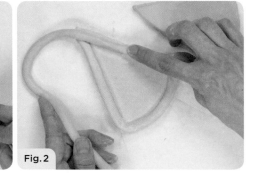

1 Pinch off a piece of clay the size of a small orange. Squeeze it flat between your hands. Flatten it further with the rolling pin or jar until it is cookie thickness.

2 With the skewer, lightly draw two diagonal lines, like a capital *A*, in the clay. The shape should resemble a triangle with a curved bottom. Use the skewer to cut out the shape. (Fig. 1)

Fig. 1

Fig. 2

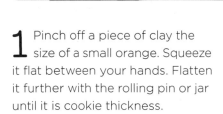

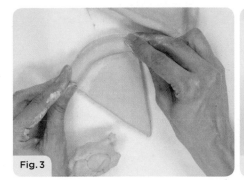
Fig. 3

Fig. 4

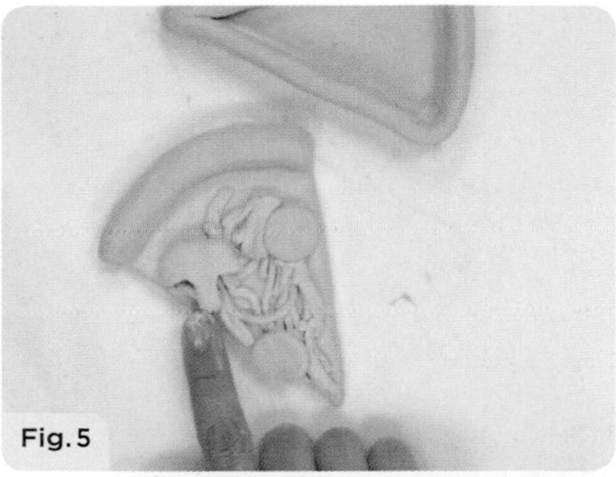

Fig. 5

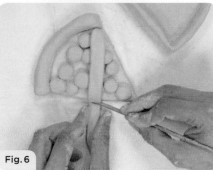
Fig. 6

Fig. 7

3 Repeat step 1. Place the triangle from step 2 on top of the slab. Trace and cut out the shape with the skewer. These pieces will be the top and bottom of the pie safe.

4 Roll long snakes of clay as thick as a finger. Use the snakes to build up the sides of the container on the bottom triangle. Use a wet toothbrush to scrub the edges of the triangle and attach each layer. (Fig. 2)

5 Continue adding layers, over-lapping the ends as you go, until the sides are the desired height and are level.

6 Use the other triangle to make the lid. For a pizza or pie slice, add a rim of clay along the short edge of the triangle for the crust. (Fig. 3)

7 For a pizza slice, squeeze clay through the garlic press to create cheese. Scrub the surface of the triangle with the toothbrush and gently press the clay "cheese" onto it. (Fig. 4 & 5)

8 Use extra clay and the skewer to cut out and add toppings, such as pepperoni, mushrooms, and peppers. Scrub the back of each topping with the wet tooth-brush and gently attach it to the top of the pizza.

9 For a fruit pie filling, make rolled balls of clay. For cake icing, see page 27. (Fig. 6)

10 Allow the top and bottom to dry for a week or more.

11 Paint the pie safe with an opaque paint, such as gouache or acrylic. When dry, coat and seal the pie safe with Mod Podge. (Fig. 7)

EGYPTIAN SARCOPHAGUS

Have you ever stopped to look at the mummies when you visited a museum? Ancient Egyptian pharaohs and queens were buried in beautiful burial boxes called *sarcophagi.* The boxes were often painted to look like the pharaoh or queen inside. For our lab, we'll use a paper-based clay called CelluClay to create our own sarcophagus and mummy!

Tools & Materials

CelluClay

large bowl

measuring cup

1 cup (235 ml) warm water

2 plastic banana split containers

gold acrylic paint

black acrylic paint

paintbrushes

1 Pull off about a quarter of the CelluClay paper pulp from the block and place it in the large bowl. Gently break it up with your fingers, until it looks like shredded paper.

2 Pour about 1 cup (235 ml) of warm water into the bowl. Knead the wet pulp until it has a clay texture. There should be no dried bits of pulp remaining. If it's too watery, knead in a little more clay. (Fig. 1)

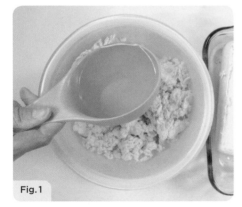

Fig. 1

Fig. 2

Fig. 3

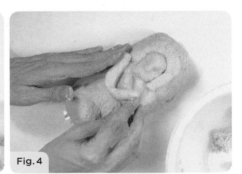
Fig. 4

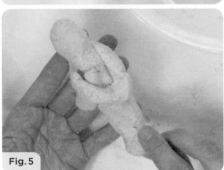
Fig. 5

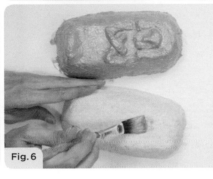
Fig. 6

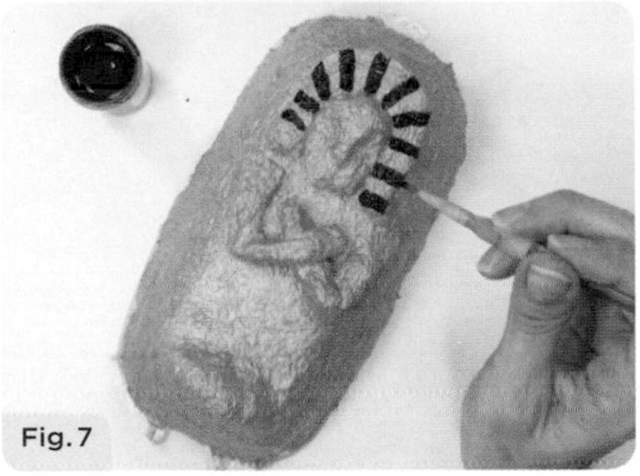

Fig. 7

3 Press clumps of the clay over the outside of the containers. Overlap bits of clay to cover both containers entirely. One will be the top of the sarcophagus and the other will be the bottom. (Fig. 2)

4 To make the head for the top of the sarcophagus, roll a piece of clay the size of a gumball. Place it a little below the top of the sarcophagus. Press your thumbs into the head shape to create eye sockets. (Fig. 3)

5 To make the headdress, roll a snake of clay. Drape it over the head.

6 To make the arms, roll two more pieces, a little thicker than the first. Place these under the head and fold them across the chest. (Fig. 4)

7 Add a lump of clay at the bottom of the sarcophagus for feet.

8 To create a mummy to place inside the sarcophagus, roll a piece of clay about as thick as a hot dog. Bend the bottom for feet. To make the arms, follow step 6. (Fig. 5)

9 Set the two sarcophagus pieces and the mummy aside to dry for several days.

10 Paint the sarcophagus gold and allow it to dry. Add details, hieroglyphs, and designs in black with a small paint brush. (Fig. 6 & 7)

MAGICAL FOREST FRIEND DOOR

Do you believe in magic? Some people say magic only enters our lives if we invite it in. What better way to invite magic in than by creating a magical forest-friend door? Place your finished door in your bedroom, next to the cookie jar, or on the stairs to the attic—you never know who might open the little door and take a step outside. In this lab, you'll use all of the skills you've learned so far to make magic happen!

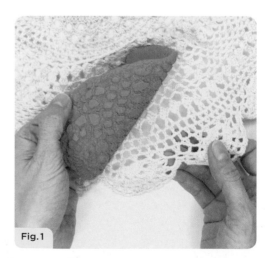

Tools & Materials

air-dry clay

textured fabric, such as burlap, lace, or doilies

rolling pin or jar

water

skewer

toothbrush

watercolor or gouache paints

paintbrushes

Mod Podge

1 Make the basic shape for the door. Break off a baseball-sized piece of air-dry clay. Flatten the clay with your hands and place it on a piece of textured fabric.

2 Roll the clay with the rolling pin or jar to make a rectangle about as thick as a cookie. Carefully peel the textured fabric from the clay. (Fig. 1)

3 Roll the bottom edge of the clay upward to create a front step for the door. If the clay dries or begins to crack, rub a little water into it with your fingers to smooth the dryness.

Fig. 1

Fig. 2

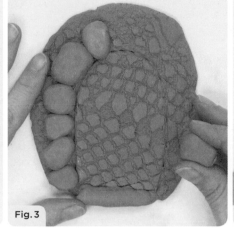

Fig. 3

Fig. 4

4 Use the skewer to lightly draw an upside down *U* for the door. (Fig. 2)

5 Roll small balls of clay and gently flatten them between your fingers. Use a wet toothbrush to attach them around the door. (Fig. 3)

6 Think of details that you can add to the door. Turn a little slab into a window, a ball into a doorknob, or a skinny snake into climbing ivy. (Fig. 4)

7 Set the finished door aside to dry for several days. You can place it on crumpled tissue or foam so air will reach underneath and help it to dry completely.

8 Paint it with watercolors or gouache paints. Try painting light colors on top of dark colors or dark colors on top of light colors for a different effect. Allow the paint to dry. Seal and protect the forest-friend door with Mod Podge. (Fig. 5)

Fig. 5

MINIATURE CACTUS GARDEN

Here's a garden that doesn't need sun or water, just your creative touch! For this lab, you'll create your own collection of potted cacti. Each of your plants will have its own little pot made from a slab of clay. Have fun exploring different textures, shapes, and sizes for your cactus garden!

Tools & Materials

air-dry clay
(I used terra cotta
colored clay.)

textured fabric,
such as lace or burlap

rolling pin or jar

water

skewer

acrylic paints in several
shades of green

paintbrushes

Mod Podge

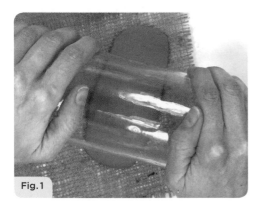

Fig. 1

1 Pinch off a Ping-Pong ball–size piece of air-dry clay. Flatten it, place it on the textured fabric, and roll it with the rolling pin. The slab should be as thick as a cookie. (Fig. 1)

Fig. 2

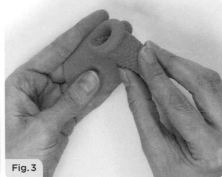
Fig. 3

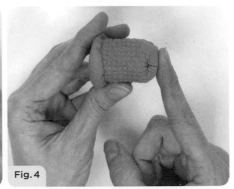
Fig. 4

Fig. 5

Fig. 6

2 Roll the bottom edge of the clay to create a rim. (Fig. 2)

3 Turn the slab into a pot by bending it into a cylinder and overlapping the ends. (Fig. 3)

4 Pinch the bottom of the cylinder to close it. Flatten the bottom by gently tapping it on the table. (Fig. 4)

5 Place a ball of clay inside the pot to act as soil for your plants.

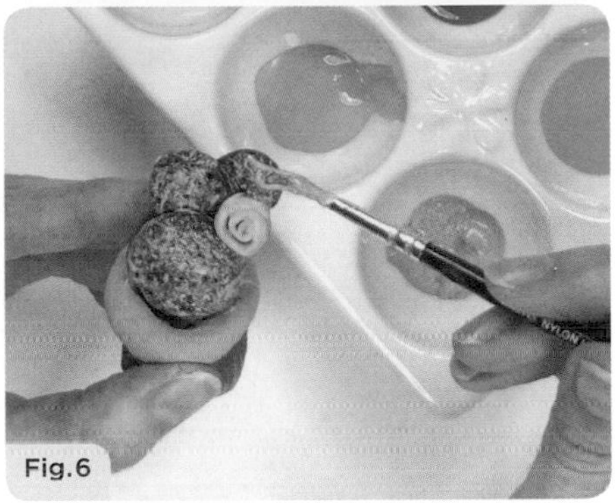

6 Look at images of cacti online. Some are shaped like flattened circles while others are like connected triangles. Flatten a piece of clay to cookie thickness and use the skewer to cut out the shapes you want.

7 Decorate the plants by poking dents in the surface with the skewer. Add them to the pots and allow them to dry for a couple of days. (Fig. 5)

8 When the cactus garden is dry, paint it different shades of green. Allow the paint to dry. Seal your cactus garden with Mod Podge. (Fig. 6)

GARDEN GNOME HOME

Gnomes are small but mighty creatures, fabled to guard Earth's treasures. This lab allows you to stretch your imagination while creating a unique and textured miniature abode.

Tools & Materials

butter knife

air-dry clay
(I used terra cotta colored clay.)

textured fabric, such as burlap, lace, doilies, or old sweaters

rolling pin or jar

skewer

toothbrush

water

watercolor, gouache, or acrylic paint
(I used watercolor paint.)

paintbrushes

Mod Podge

1 Use the butter knife to cut two 1" (2.5 cm) slabs of clay.

2 Lay out the textured fabric. Place the clay on top of the fabric and press it down firmly. Use the rolling pin to roll the clay flat to cookie thickness. (Fig. 1)

3 Peel the clay from the fabric and set it aside. Repeat steps 1 and 2 for the second piece.

4 Make the roof for the house. Take one of the pieces from step 2 and fold it into a cone, narrow at the top and wide at the bottom, with the texture on the outside. Set it aside. (Fig. 2)

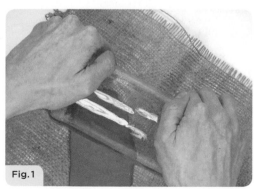

Fig.1

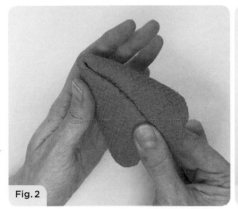

Fig. 2

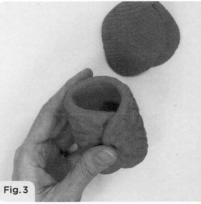

Fig. 3

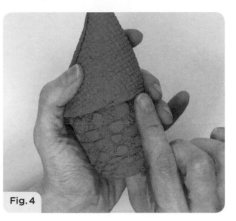

Fig. 4

5 Now take the other piece from step 2 and bend it into a cylinder. The top and bottom should have the same size opening, with the texture on the outside. This will be the bottom part of the house. (Fig. 3)

6 Gently place the cone roof on the house. If it doesn't fit, simply shape the cylinder again to make it narrower. Use a toothbrush and water to attach the roof to the house. Use your fingers to smooth and attach the two pieces together. (Fig. 4)

7 Now use your imagination to decorate the gnome home! What kind of door will you make? How about a window with a flower box? Use the skewer to scratch the outlines of a door or window into the clay. Add a chimney with another piece of clay. Allow the gnome home to dry for several days in a safe place.

8 Paint the gnome home with watercolor, gouache, or acrylic paint. I like to layer different colors so the textures are more visible. Allow the paint to dry. Seal the gnome home with Mod Podge. (Fig. 5)

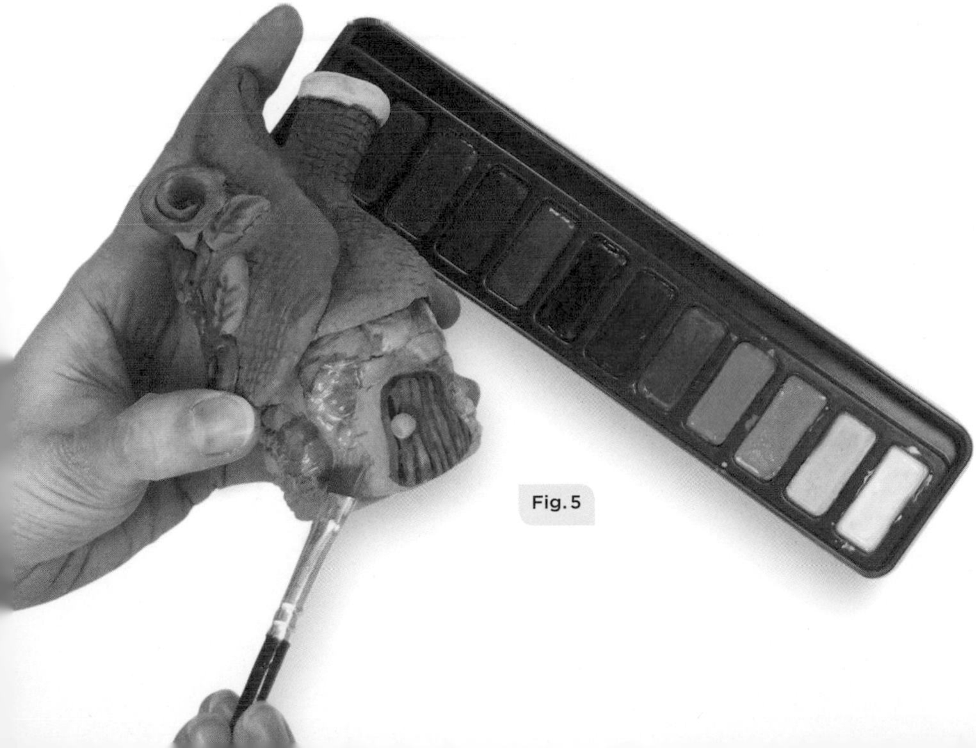

Fig. 5

BOBBLEHEAD PETS

To create a bobblehead pet, you'll use the skills you learned in earlier labs for pinch pots and textures. You can create any bobblehead creature you can imagine, from a couple of sweet owls, like I've made here, to monsters or dragons.

MAKE THE BASE OF THE BOBBLEHEAD

The base is made as a cylinder with a pointed top for the head to bobble on.

Tools & Materials

dull knife

air-dry clay

textured fabric,
such as burlap

rolling pin or jar

ruler

skewer

toothbrush

water

watercolor, gouache,
or acrylic paint

paintbrushes

Mod Podge

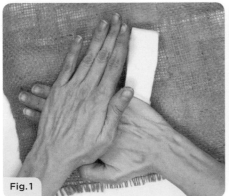

Fig. 1

Fig. 2

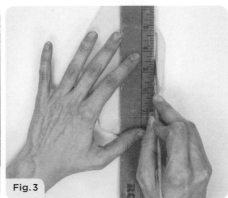

Fig. 3

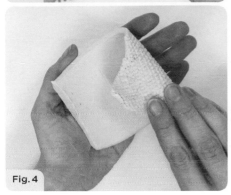

Fig. 4

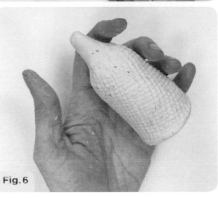

Fig. 5

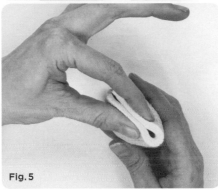

Fig. 6

1 Cut about 2" (5 cm) of clay from the short side of the clay block. Lay it on a piece of textured fabric and press it down to flatten it. (Fig. 1)

2 Use the rolling pin to flatten the clay some more. Roll it up and down and side to side until it is cookie thickness.

3 Peel the clay off of the fabric. Lay it texture-side up on your work surface. (Fig. 2)

4 Using a ruler and skewer, measure and cut the clay into a rectangle about 4" × 7" (10 × 18 cm). (Fig. 3)

5 Lift the clay and bend it into a cylinder shape, overlapping the short ends. Use the skewer to slip and score the clay to hold the seam in place. (Fig. 4)

6 Pinch around the top edge of the cylinder to start shaping it into a point. Continue pinching until the point is ½" (1.25 cm) long and about as thick as an uncapped marker. If it is too thin, it may break when dry. (Fig. 5 & 6)

MAKE THE BOBBLEHEAD

1 Roll a ball of clay the size of a golf ball.

2 Create a pinch pot as shown in Lab 2, pages 22 and 23. Place the ball in the palm of your hand and cup your fingers around it. Press the thumb of your other hand deeply into the ball. (Fig. 7)

3 Set the ball indented-side up on your work surface. Use your fingers to create a hollow head, pinching the clay to cookie thickness all the way around. (Fig. 8)

4 Turn the head over and set it on top of the base to make sure it fits. Remove the head and place it on your work surface.

Fig. 7

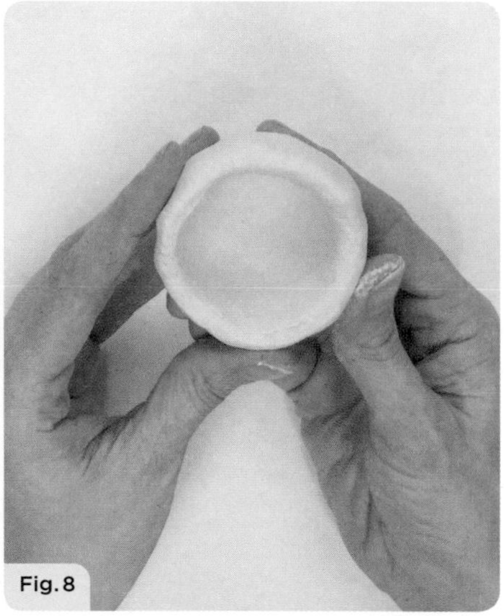

Fig. 8

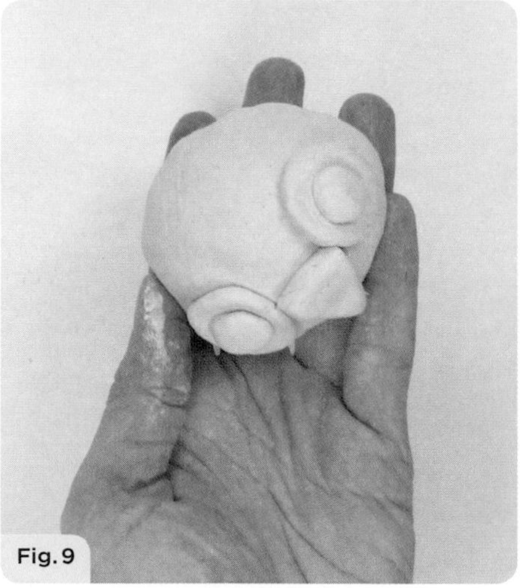

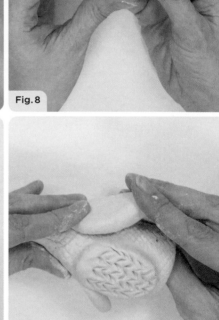

Fig. 9

Fig. 10

5 Now make the bobblehead's face. Using additional clay, roll balls for the eyes, cut a triangle shape for the nose, and add texture with the skewer. Attach the pieces by the slip-and-score method (page 11) with the wet toothbrush or skewer. (Fig. 9)

6 Add details to the body of the bobblehead. Use additional clay to create wings, feet, and a belly. The possibilities are endless! (Fig. 10 & 11)

7 Allow the bobblehead pet to dry for a couple of days. When it is no longer cool to the touch, it's dry.

8 Paint your creation with watercolor, gouache, or acrylic paint. Allow the paint to dry. Seal and protect your creation with Mod Podge. (Fig. 12 & 13)

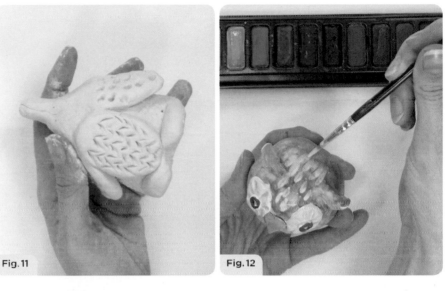

Fig. 11

Fig. 12

Fig. 13

Long ago, castles or even entire towns were built on hilltops with moats around them. A moat is a body of water that surrounds an area. Moats were built to provide protection for the townspeople living inside the walls of the castle. You can create your very own castle on a hill complete with a surrounding moat in this lab.

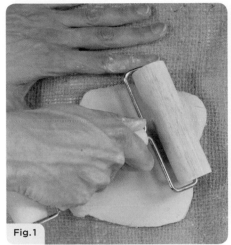

Fig. 1

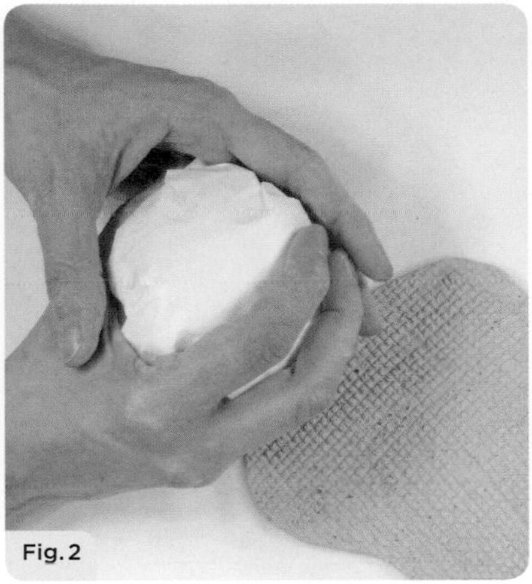

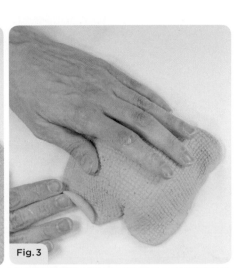

Fig. 2

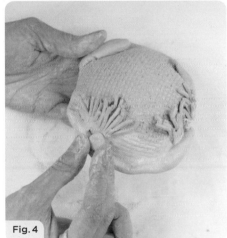

Fig. 3

Fig. 4

1 Cut a 12" (30.5 cm)-long
piece of dental floss and pull
it tightly between your hands.
Use the dental floss to cut a toast-
thick slice from the brick of clay.

2 Lay a piece of textured fabric
on your work surface. Place
the slab of clay on top. Roll or
pound the clay to a level cookie
thickness. Peel the slab from the
fabric and place it texture-side up
on your work surface. (Fig. 1)

3 Crumble a piece of newspaper into a ball the size
of a small orange. Flatten one
side by pressing it onto your
work surface. Drape the slab of
clay, texture-side up, over the
newspaper so that it forms a
hill. (Fig. 2)

4 Gently roll the edges of the
clay toward the hill, creating
a moat. (Fig. 3)

5 Squeeze several small pieces
of clay through a garlic press
to create grass for the moat's
shore. Roll small balls of clay for
rocks. Scrub the moat's shore
with a wet toothbrush and attach
the grass and rocks. (Fig. 4)

6 To create the castle, flatten another piece of clay to cookie thickness. Using the ruler and skewer, measure and cut the clay into a rectangle. Mine measures 3½" × 7" (9 × 18 cm).

7 Bend the short sides of the rectangle inward to make a cylinder. To attach, scrub the edges with a wet toothbrush. Overlap the two pieces of clay and smooth with your finger and water. (Fig. 5)

8 Create castle turrets at the top of the cylinder by using the skewer to cut out small rectangles. Reuse the small triangles by attaching them to the sides of the cylinder to look like building stones. (Fig. 6 & 7)

9 To create a door, use the skewer to cut an upside down *L* at the bottom of the cylinder. Gently pull the L outward to open the door. (Fig. 8)

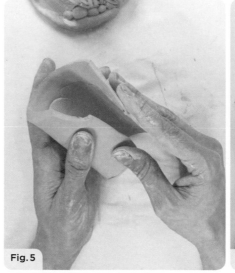
Fig. 5

Fig. 6

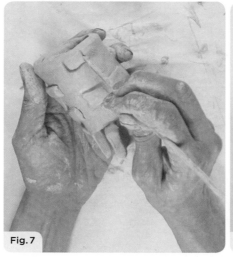
Fig. 7

Fig. 8

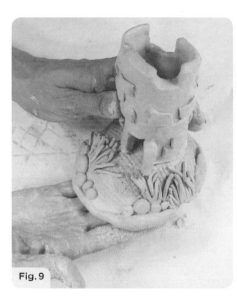

Fig. 9

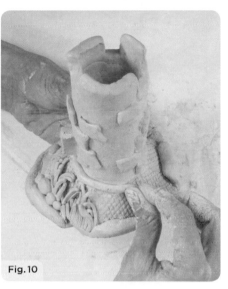

Fig. 10

10 Attach the castle to the top of the hill with a little water. To secure it, roll a snake of clay to go around the base. Scratch the surface of the castle and hill with a wet toothbrush and attach the snake of clay. (Fig. 9 & 10)

11 Further embellish the castle with bits of clay for ivy and more stones. Allow it to dry for up to a week.

12 Use watercolor or gouache to paint the castle, hill, and moat. Allow the paint to dry. Coat your creation with Mod Podge. (Fig. 11)

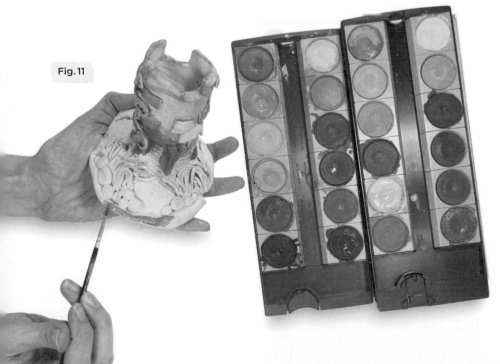

Fig. 11

CRAYON AND PENCIL SCULPTURE

Imagine that you had a giant crayon or pencil. How fun would that be? Many artists draw inspiration from familiar objects when creating their art. This form of art is called *pop art.* The word *pop* comes from *popular culture*, or items that surround us in everyday. Pencils and crayons are a part of everyday life, so why not use them as subjects for a big pop art sculpture?

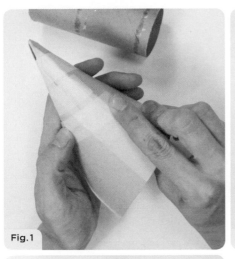

Fig. 1

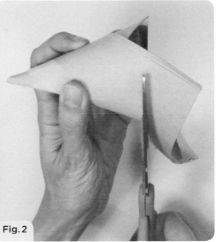

Fig. 2

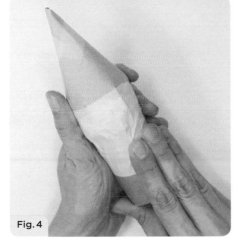

Fig. 3

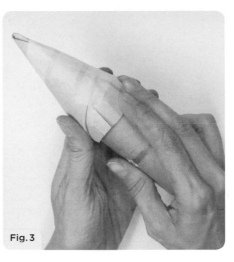

Fig. 4

1 Create the tip of the crayon or pencil by bending the cardboard into a cone. Pull the upper-right corner toward the center of the cardboard. The widest part should be about the width of the paper towel roll. Tape the cardboard to hold the shape. (Fig. 1)

2 The bottom of the cone will be uneven. Use the scissors to trim it so that the edge is flat. (Fig. 2)

3 Make cuts about every ½" (1.3 cm) around the bottom of the cone so that it fits over the opening of the towel roll. (Fig. 3)

4 Tape the cone to one end of the roll. Also place a large piece of tape across the opposite end of the paper towel roll to close it off. (Fig. 4)

5 Following the manufacturer's directions, mix up a batch of CelluClay with the water in the bowl. You'll need a ball of clay about as big as a baseball. CelluClay can be very dusty, so it's best to mix it in the kitchen or outdoors.

6 Flatten small balls of clay between your hands. Lay them onto the sculpture. Overlap additional pieces slightly when adding more. Continue until the entire sculpture is covered. (Fig. 5 & 6)

7 If it's a sunny day, place the sculpture outside on a sheet of wax paper. Otherwise, allow it to dry indoors for up to a week.

8 If you're making a pencil, draw a line around the tip for the pencil lead. Draw a line around where the point meets the paper towel roll to indicate the wood portion of the pencil. Draw additional lines to indicate the metal band and eraser at the end of the pencil. Paint the different sections with the appropriate colors and allow the paint to dry. (Fig. 7–9)

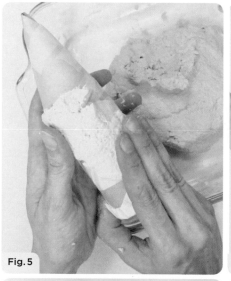

Fig. 5

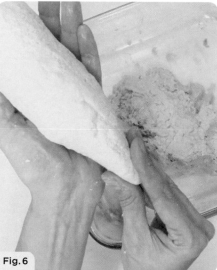

Fig. 6

Fig. 7

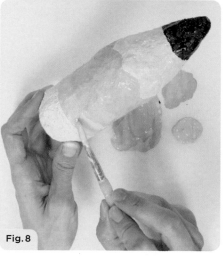

Fig. 8

Fig. 9

Fig. 10

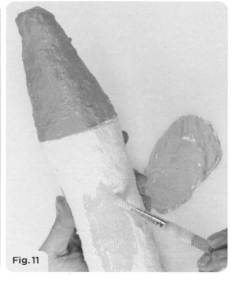

Fig. 11

9 If you're making a crayon, draw a line where the cone at the top meets the paper towel roll. This will be where the crayon's wrapper starts.

Fig. 12

Draw another line around the opposite end of the crayon to show where the paper wrapper ends. Paint the crayon the color of your choice and allow the paint to dry. (Fig. 10 & 11)

10 Brush on a coat of Mod Podge to add a little shine. (Fig. 12)

WOODLAND CREATURE PORTRAITS

I live near a forest and share my backyard with many woodland creatures. In the morning, bunnies bounce by in search of the perfect blades of grass. During the day, squirrels and chipmunks visit our bird feeder. At night, deer like to rest under a tree while raccoons knock over our trashcan. It's fun to have all of these furry friends nearby. They are the inspiration behind these woodland creature portraits, which you'll make with modeling clay.

Tools & Materials

air-dry clay
(I used Plus
Modeling Clay.)

water

skewer

cardboard

scissors

acrylic paint in gold
and brown

paintbrushes

watercolors

Mod Podge

glue

1 Pinch off a Ping-Pong ball–size piece of clay and roll it into a ball. Use your fingers to pinch and shape the clay to create a muzzle—that's a nose—for your animal. A fox or deer has a long muzzle. A bunny or squirrel has a shorter one. (Fig. 1)

2 Press your thumbs into the clay to create the eye sockets. (Fig. 2)

3 Stretch and pull the clay to create ears for your animal. Depending on the animal, the ears might be long or short, and they might start at the top of the head or on the sides. If your clay starts to dry out and crack, work a little water into the clay. (Fig. 3)

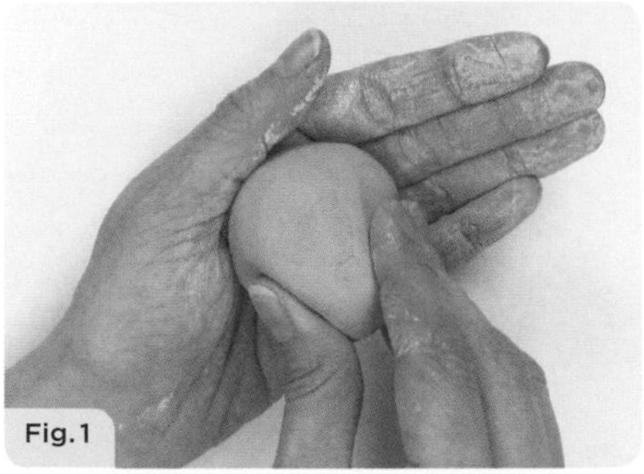

Fig. 1

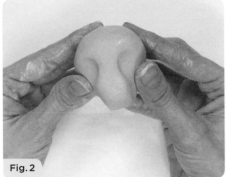

Fig. 2

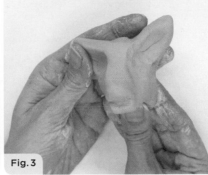

Fig. 3

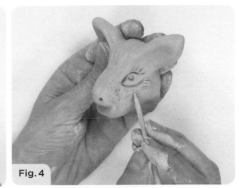

Fig. 4

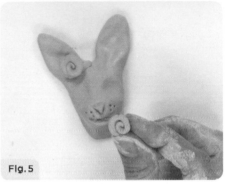

Fig. 5

4 Hold the skewer horizontally and use the point to make an opening for the animal's mouth.

5 Now use the point of the skewer to scratch fur on the animal's head. Poke holes for nostrils and whiskers. Then gently draw the eyes and other details. (Fig. 4)

6 To give the creature a little character, add a bowtie or decorate its head with flowers and leaves. If you're making a deer, poke a couple of holes in the top of the head so you can add twigs for antlers. Set the animal portrait aside to dry for several days. (Fig. 5)

7 While the clay is drying, cut out shapes from cardboard to use as mounts. Paint the mounts with gold and brown acrylic paint to make the faux wood background. Allow the paint to dry.

8 Paint the animals with layers of watercolors to create a furry textured look. Allow the paint to dry. (Fig. 6)

9 Paint the animals with Mod Podge. Once dry, glue the animal portrait to the faux wood base and display!

Fig. 6

VIKING SHIPS

The Vikings sailed in wooden boats called *longships*, which often had the head of a dragon at the front and the tail at the back. Vikings arranged their shields along the outside of the ship both for protection and to conserve space. Often, the sails featured symbolic designs.

Tools & Materials

air-dry clay
(I used DAS air-dry
modeling clay.)

toothbrush

water

skewer

gouache or acrylic paint

paintbrushes

paper

scissors

pencils or crayons

glue

Mod Podge

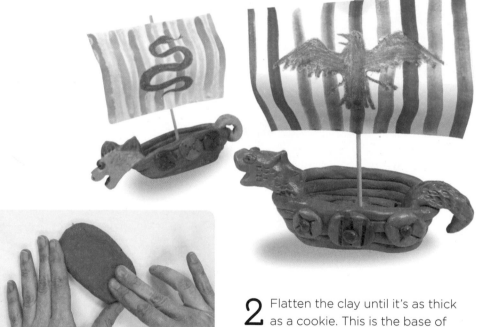

Fig. 1

1 Pinch off a piece of clay the size of a golf ball. Roll it into a ball and then roll it into a hotdog shape, about 4" (10 cm) long.

2 Flatten the clay until it's as thick as a cookie. This is the base of the ship. (Fig. 1)

3 Build the ship taller by the coil method. Begin with a piece of clay the size of a gumball. Roll it between your hands to make a snake of clay as thick as a finger. (Fig. 2)

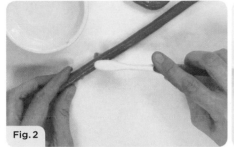

Fig. 2

Fig. 3

Fig. 4

Fig. 5

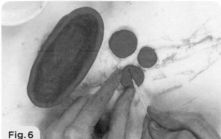

Fig. 6

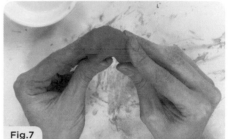

Fig. 7

Fig. 8

Fig. 9

4 Attach the snake of clay to the edge of the ship base using the wet toothbrush method. Continue adding layers until the ship is the desired height. (Fig. 3 & 4)

5 Make the ship narrower by gently pressing in the sides. Make it a bit longer by gently pulling at the ends. (Fig. 5)

6 To make shields, roll and flatten small balls of clay. Use the skewer to decorate the shields. Use the wet toothbrush to attach the shields to the ship. (Fig. 6)

7 Create the ship's dragon head with a thick piece of clay snake. Use the skewer to create nostrils and eyes. Pinch the clay to create

spikes. Use the dull end of the skewer to create scales. Create a tail by the same method. (Fig. 7)

8 Attach the dragon head and tail to the ship with the wet toothbrush. (Fig. 8)

9 Poke a hole in the center of the boat. This is where the mast will be glued. Allow the ship to dry for up to a week. Paint it when it's dry.

10 Cut out a paper sail. Draw or paint a design on it. (Fig. 9)

11 Glue the top of the skewer upright into the hole in the ship. Allow it to dry. Poke a tiny hole at the top and bottom of the sail and slide it onto the skewer.

12 Seal and protect the Viking ship with Mod Podge.

MARIONETTE PUPPETS

air-dry clay
(I used paper clay.)

water

skewer

acrylic paint

paintbrushes

toilet paper tube, one
per marionette

hole punch

yarn or twine

two twigs 10" or 12"
(25.5 or 30.5 cm) long

glue

A marionette is a puppet that seems to come to life when you move its strings. Create marionettes in the forms of animals and people and perform your very own show!

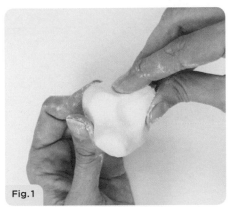

Fig. 1

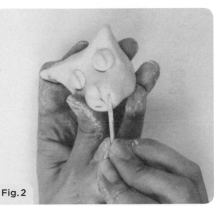

Fig. 2

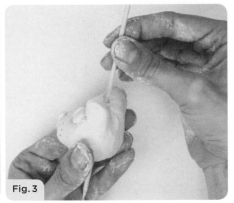

Fig. 3

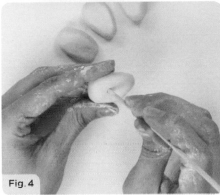

Fig. 4

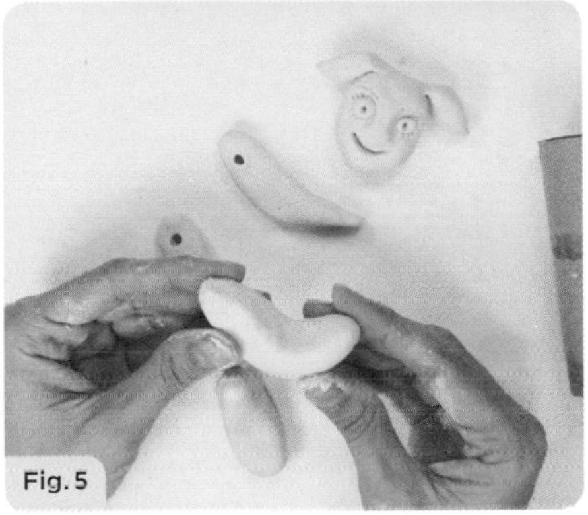

Fig. 5

1 Create the marionette's head by rolling a piece of clay the size of a Ping-Pong ball. If you're creating an animal, gently pinch the clay forward to create a muzzle, as in Lab 21 (page 68). Create ears either by pinching and pulling the clay or by sculpting the ears separately and attaching them with water. Press your thumbs into the clay to make eye sockets. (Fig. 1 & 2)

2 If you're creating a person, create the eyes and nose separately and attach them with a little water.

3 Use the skewer to poke a hole through the head, going from the top to the bottom. Twist the skewer back and forth while gently pushing it through. Set the head aside. (Fig. 3)

4 If you're making an animal, make the feet by rolling four small pieces of clay into balls. Use the skewer to poke a hole through each of the balls. Allow the feet to dry. (Fig. 4)

5 If you're making a person, roll out four little tube shapes for the arms and legs. Use the skewer to poke a hole through each limb from side to side. Allow the limbs to dry. (Fig. 5)

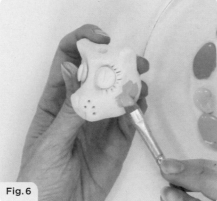

Fig. 6

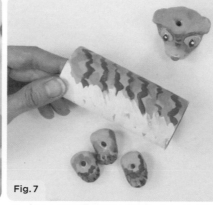

Fig. 7

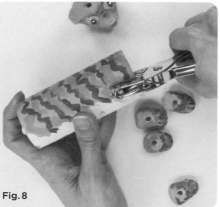

Fig. 8

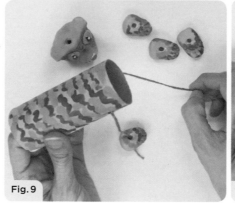

Fig. 9

Fig. 10

6 When the pieces have dried, you're ready to paint. You'll need the paper tube, too—it will form the marionette's body. Gather all the pieces, decide on the colors, and paint the head, feet/limbs, and body with acrylic paint. Allow the paint to dry. (Fig. 6 & 7)

7 To assemble an animal, punch two holes at the front of the tube and two holes in the same positions at the back. Thread yarn or twine through the punched holes on the front of the animal's body. Now thread the yarn or twine through one of the feet and tie a double knot at the bottom to secure. Do the same for the other foot. Repeat this process for the back of the animal's body. (Fig. 8 & 9)

8 To attach the animal's head, punch a hole in the tube above one set of feet. Cut two lengths of yarn or twine about 18" (45.5 cm) long. Double knot one end of the yarn. Thread the yarn through the hole inside the tube so that the knot is on the inside. Slide the animal head down the string from the top. (Fig. 10)

9 Punch a hole above the feet at the opposite end of the tube. Double knot the end of the other piece of string. Thread it through the hole as before, knotting it where it emerges from the hole. This string and the one attached to the head will control the puppet.

Fig. 11

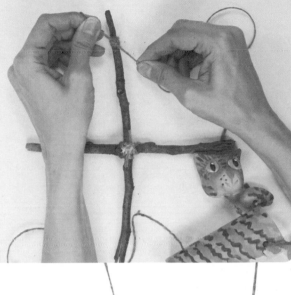

Fig. 12

10 If you're making a person, follow steps 8 and 9, adding the arms outside the tube and the legs inside. To attach the head, punch two holes directly above the holes created for the arms. Using a 26" (66 cm) piece of yarn, thread it through both holes. Bring the strings together and tie a double knot. Slide the head over the two strings.

11 Make the marionette controls by tying two twigs together in a cross. Glue the knot to secure it and let dry. Tie and knot a string around the intersection of the two sticks to secure it. (Fig. 11)

12 If you're making an animal, tie the ends of the yarn pieces to two ends of the cross stick with a double knot. Add a dot of glue to the knots and allow it to dry before operating. (Fig. 12)

13 If you're making a person, attach the doubled string to the center of the cross sticks. Tie a double knot, anchor it with glue, and let dry.

ANIMAL MASQUERADE MASKS

During a holiday called *Carnival*, celebrated around the world, there are days of parties and parades. People enjoy going to these events wearing fun masks to hide their identities. Make your own carnival mask and see whether anyone recognizes you!

Tools & Materials

CelluClay

water

large bowl

plastic mask

poster board

scissors

masking tape

pencil

acrylic paint

paintbrushes

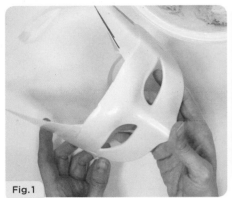

Fig. 1

Fig. 2

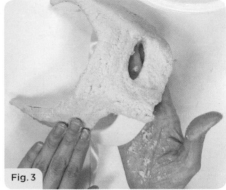

Fig. 3

1 Following the steps in Lab 14 (pages 48–49), mix the CelluClay with water in the bowl.

2 Set out the masks. Using poster board and scissors, cut out shapes for animal ears. Triangles would be perfect for a fox or a cat. Round ears work well for a panda. Tape the ears to the masks. (Fig. 1)

3 Press the clay mixture over the entire mask evenly. Smooth it with your fingers. (Fig. 2)

4 Smooth more clay over the ears. Set the mask aside and allow it to dry for several days. (Fig. 3)

5 Draw an animal face design on the mask and paint it. When the paint has dried, celebrate by hosting a masquerade ball! (Fig. 4 & 5)

Fig. 4

Fig. 5

POLYMER CLAY AND LEARNING THE BASICS

~~~~~~~

Polymer clay is a wonderful

medium to explore. Because it is not water based, it is less messy than other clays. And no matter what you want to make, there's a polymer clay color to match. However, you don't need to purchase them all. In this unit, you'll learn that a lot of the fun of working with polymer clay is in marbling or blending colors. Like the other types of clay previously explored, polymer clay is great for grabbing texture.

CRYSTALLIZED PINCH POTS

The magic of this lab is that you'll be a scientist as well as an artist when you try it! You're going to grow crystals inside your clay pinch pot. You'll be amazed at the beautiful results of this science experiment.

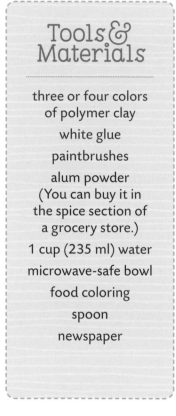

Tools & Materials

three or four colors of polymer clay

white glue

paintbrushes

alum powder
(You can buy it in the spice section of a grocery store.)

1 cup (235 ml) water

microwave-safe bowl

food coloring

spoon

newspaper

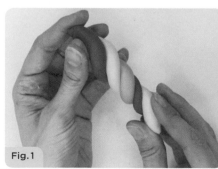

Fig. 1

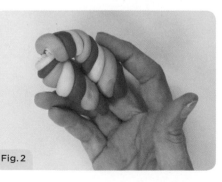

Fig. 2

1 Pinch off a gumball-size piece of each color of clay. Roll them into snakes of equal length.

2 Twist the snakes together, and then form them into a ball. (Fig. 1 & 2)

Fig. 3

Fig. 4

Fig. 5

Fig. 6

Fig. 7

3 Roll the ball of clay into a snake. Twist it again and form it into a ball. You can repeat this as often as you'd like. The more times the clay is rolled, twisted, and formed into a ball, the more the colors will swirl. (Fig. 3)

4 Place the ball of clay in your palm. Press your thumb deep inside it and then pinch the edges to create a small pot. Bake the pot in the oven according to the manufacturer's directions. Allow it to cool. (Fig. 4)

5 When the pot has cooled, paint a layer of glue inside it. Sprinkle alum powder onto the wet glue until it is covered. Allow the glue to dry for several hours. (Fig. 5)

6 Pour the water into the bowl and bring it to a boil in the microwave. Add ½ cup (110 grams) of alum powder and again, bring it to a boil. Stir a few drops of food coloring into the mixture. Stir the mixture and allow it to cool. (Fig. 6 & 7)

7 Place your pinch pot in the solution and allow it to sit overnight. In the morning, gently remove the pot from the solution and place it on newspaper to dry. Enjoy the sparkles!

8 You can save and reuse the alum powder solution. Simply reheat it in the microwave until the alum powder has dissolved. Results of this experiment may vary from very large to very small crystals.

COLOR MIXING CLOCK

LAB 26

You don't have to own every rainbow color of polymer clay. You can make them yourself from the three primary colors—red, yellow, and blue. In this lab, you'll use twelve different colors to make the numbers on a clock. You'll need a battery-powered clock kit, which comes with numbers and hands. These can be found at craft and hardware stores and are very easy to assemble.

Tools & Materials

dull knife

polymer clay in red, yellow, and blue

discarded CD

battery-powered clock-making kit

1 Cut two small pieces of clay from each of the three colors. Roll each piece into a ball. Place them on a table to form a triangle. These are the three primary colors. (Fig. 1)

2 To create the secondary colors, combine the primaries: red and yellow to make orange; yellow and blue for green; and red and blue for purple. (See box opposite.)

3 Cut gumball-size pieces of red and yellow from the polymer

blocks. Individually, roll each color into a snake. Starting at the top, twist two colors together. Squeeze the twist into a ball. Roll it into a snake again, twist it, and squeeze it into a ball. Watch the colors blend to make orange. Repeat until the clay is the color you want. Use the same process to make green and purple. (Fig. 2 & 3)

Fig. 1

Fig. 2

Fig. 3

Fig. 4

Fig. 5

Fig. 6

4 To make the tertiary colors, blend the primary and secondary colors. See the box below right.

5 Make a small ball of each color about the size of a gumball. Place the CD shiny-side up on your work surface. Arrange the balls, equally spaced, around the edge of the CD. Press them into place. Gently press the numbers of the clock into the clay. (Fig. 4–6)

6 Bake the clock at a slightly lower temperature than recommended in the manufacturer's

directions. This will bake the clay—without melting the numbers or the CD. Let cool when done.

7 Assemble the clock's mechanism according to the directions that come with the kit.

Start with Three Colors, End with Twelve!

Primary Colors
1. red
2. yellow
3. blue

Secondary Colors
4. orange (red + yellow)
5. green (blue + yellow)
6. purple (blue + red)

Tertiary Colors
7. red-orange (red + orange)
8. yellow-orange (yellow + orange)
9. yellow-green (yellow + green)
10. blue-green (blue + green)
11. blue-purple (blue + purple)
12. red-purple (red + purple)

LAB 27 FUN FORTUNE COOKIES

When you eat at a Chinese restaurant, you are served fortune cookies with tea at the end of the meal. Our clay version of a fortune cookie will make a sweet gift for a family member or friend. Be sure to write a happy fortune for someone special to discover.

Tools & Materials

polymer clay,
in brown and white

small strips of paper

markers or pens

jewelry hoop,
optional

You will see a unicorn.

Look for magic.

You are sunshine.

Today, pizza!

Rainbows follow you.

1 Start with the fortunes. Write some fun fortunes or kind words on small strips of paper. (Fig. 1)

2 Now make the cookies. For a light brown cookie color, roll out snakes of brown and white polymer clay. Twist the two snakes together and then form them into a ball. Continue to do this until the colors are well blended. End with the clay in a ball.

3 Flatten the ball between your fingers. Press the clay onto your work surface and flatten it into a circle. (Fig. 2)

4 With your fingers tucked inside, bend the clay up like a taco. Keep your fingers inside to create a pocket in the clay and give the cookie a three-dimensional shape.

Fig. 1

Fig. 2

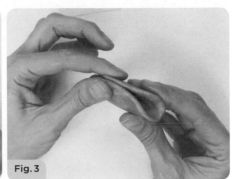

Fig. 3

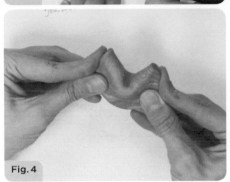

Fig. 4

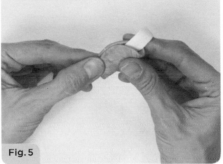

Fig. 5

5 Gently pinch around the top and one side of the taco shape. Leave one side open. That is where the fortune will slide in. (Fig. 3)

6 Starting from the pinched edge, gently bend the two ends of the cookie toward each other until the inside is a *V* shape. (Fig. 4)

7 Bake the clay cookie according to the manufacturer's directions. When cool, slide the fortune inside and deliver it to a friend!

Fig. 6

VARIATIONS

1 Follow steps 1 through 3. Before folding the clay into a taco shape, place a thinly flattened piece of white clay on top of it, just to one side of the center. Allow the white clay to hang out of one end of the cookie just a little. Then follow steps 4 through 7. The white clay will have the appearance of paper. (Fig. 5)

2 Add a small jewelry hoop to the cookie before it's baked and use it as a charm for a necklace. (Fig. 6)

LIGHT-UP LIGHTNING BUGS

Some people call them lightning bugs; others call them fireflies. No matter what you call them, during the summer months, these small insects light up the night. They are beautiful to watch and even more fun to create.

1 Roll a small piece of clay between your hands to make a ball. Shape the ball into an oval about ½" (1.3 cm) long.

2 Create the wings of the insect by using the skewer to cut the oval in half lengthwise. Gently separate these two pieces and flatten to form wings. (Fig. 1)

3 Roll a small ball of clay for the bug's head. Attach the wings to the head. (Fig. 2)

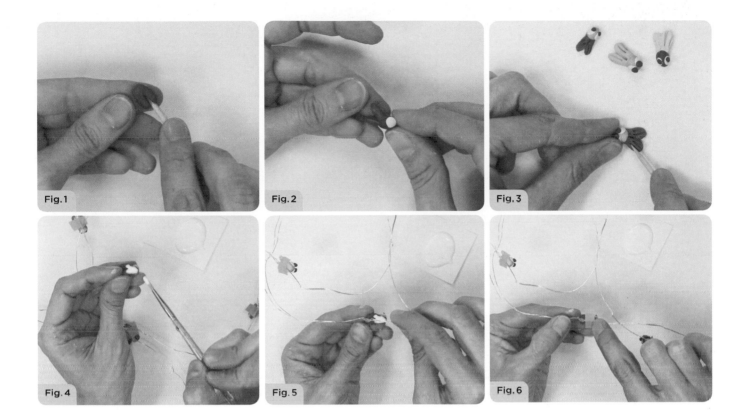

Fig. 1

Fig. 2

Fig. 3

Fig. 4

Fig. 5

Fig. 6

4 Roll two tiny white balls of clay and press them into the bug's head for eyes. Add even smaller balls of black clay to the eyes for the pupils.

5 Create as many lightning bugs as there are lights or as many as desired. (Fig. 3)

6 Follow the manufacturer's instructions to bake the clay bugs. Once they've cooled, cut pieces of paper about the same size as the bugs and set aside.

7 Brush a dollop of glue to the back of each bug. Position each bug on the strand of lights so it has a bulb near its backside. (Fig. 4)

8 Place a piece of the cut paper over the back of the bug so that the light is sandwiched in between. Press gently so as not to break the bug and count to 30. This will allow time for the glue to set. (Fig. 5 & 6)

9 Once all of the bugs have been added, light up the lightning bugs! For fun, keep these on display in a glass jar and use as a light on a nightstand.

ALL-ABOUT-ME MOBILE

A mobile is a sculpture that moves and changes its form when it's hung in the air. Gather treasures from outside to attach to your mobile. Watch your work of art shift and transform while it moves.

Tools & Materials

sticks, feathers, leaves

acrylic paint

paintbrushes

polymer clay, in three or four colors

skewer

cookie cutters (optional)

small metal clay stamps (optional)

yarn or string

12" (30.5 cm)-long stick

glue

1 Collect items from outside, such as sticks, feathers, and leaves. Paint lines, designs, and patterns on these treasures.

2 Follow the steps in Lab 25 (pages 80–81) to create blended clay with your favorite colors. Roll them into small balls and flatten some of them. (Fig. 1)

Fig. 1

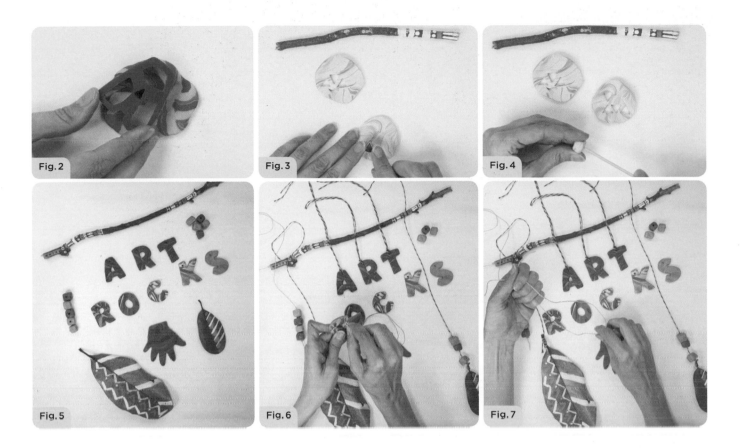

Fig. 2

Fig. 3

Fig. 4

Fig. 5

Fig. 6

Fig. 7

3 Use the skewer or cookie cutters to cut shapes into the clay. Add designs with a metal stamp, if desired. (Fig. 2 & 3)

4 Use the skewer to poke a hole at the top of each shape. Poke holes through the remaining small balls to make beads. (Fig. 4)

5 Bake the clay, including the balls still on the skewer, according to the manufacturer's directions. Allow the clay to cool.

6 Lay out the mobile design. To string the beads, cut a 10" (25.5 cm) length of yarn. Make a double knot at one end. Slide the beads down the string until the knot stops them. Tie the string to the hanging stick with a double knot. (Fig. 5)

7 To add the other designs, cut a piece of yarn double the length of the bead yarn. Fold it in half. Place the folded yarn inside the hole of each piece. This will

create a loop of yarn. Thread the ends of the yarn through each loop. Secure it to the hanging stick with a double knot. (Fig. 6)

8 To add leaves and feathers, attach yarn with a double knot. Secure them to the hanging stick with a drop of glue on all of the knots. Let dry. (Fig. 7)

9 To hang, cut a long piece of string and tie it to the ends of the hanging stick with a double knot.

POLYMER CLAY SCULPTURE

~~~~~~~~~~

Now that you know how to

explore color and texture in polymer clay, let's dive into sculpting. Because polymer clay is more expensive than other clays, sculptures created from polymer clays are smaller. However, many of the labs previously covered in this book could also be created in polymer clay. In this unit, you'll learn how to work on a smaller scale and also how to create the structures underneath a sculpture.

LAB
30

TIE-DYE TURTLES

In this lab, you'll explore a fun technique that creates the colors and patterns of a tie-dye T-shirt. The funky design could be added to many of your sculptures. Today you'll be adding it to a rock and turning it into a turtle!

Tools & Materials

round rocks

polymer clay, in several colors

skewer

1 Walk outside and collect a few rocks that are round in shape. The rocks do not have to be smooth. Wash and dry them. (Fig. 1)

2 Work an entire block of clay between your hands until it's soft and easy to squeeze. The color you use does not matter because it will not be seen.

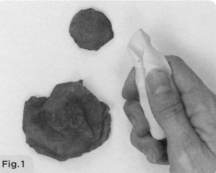

Fig. 1

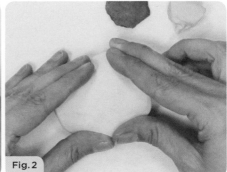

Fig. 2

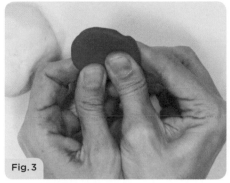

Fig. 3

Fig. 4

Fig. 5

Fig. 6

3 Roll the softened clay into a ball and flatten it into a thin circle. Cover the upper part of the rock with the clay. Only the bottom of the rock should be exposed. Patch on pieces of flattened clay, if needed, to cover the areas, so that there is a smooth surface for the turtle's back. (Fig. 2)

4 To create the tie-dye, pick a polymer color and roll it into a ball the size of a large gumball. Flatten it into a thin circle with your fingers. (Fig. 3)

5 Repeat, making a slightly smaller circle of clay with another color. Center it on the larger circle of clay. With your finger, smear the colors of the inner circle to the outer. (Fig. 4)

6 Pick another color, roll it into a smaller ball, and flatten it. Center it on top of the other colors and smear the inner circle to the previous circle. Do not smear all the way to the first circle.

7 Continue adding smaller circles and smearing with shorter strokes. Once complete, drape your tie-dye over the rock and tuck it underneath. (Fig. 5)

8 Roll out four small pieces of clay the size of a peanut for the turtle's feet. Attach two on each side. (Fig. 6)

9 To create a head, roll a thick coil of clay and bend into a cane shape. Attach it to the rock. Use the skewer to press into the clay to create the mouth. Roll tiny balls of clay for the eyes and pupils and attach. (Fig. 7)

10 Follow the manufacturer's directions for baking the clay turtle, leaving the rock inside. Allow the turtle to cool thoroughly before touching it.

Fig. 7

An accordion book gets its name because it can expand just like the musical instrument. The book's paper is folded back and forth, like a zigzag that can open to be quite long. The accordion book was invented in Asia for folding scrolls that had become too long to be rolled. You can create a unique accordion book to hold all your interesting ideas!

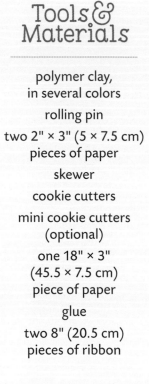

Tools & Materials

polymer clay, in several colors

rolling pin

two 2" × 3" (5 × 7.5 cm) pieces of paper

skewer

cookie cutters

mini cookie cutters (optional)

one 18" × 3" (45.5 × 7.5 cm) piece of paper

glue

two 8" (20.5 cm) pieces of ribbon

1 Follow the steps in Lab 26 (pages 82–83) to blend two or three pieces of clay together for a swirled effect. Flatten the clay until it is slightly bigger than one of the 2" × 3" (5 × 7.5 cm) pieces of paper.

2 Place the paper on top of the flattened clay and trace it with a skewer, cutting the clay into a rectangle. Repeat steps 1 and 2. One piece of clay will serve as the book's cover and the other as the back. (Fig. 1)

Fig. 1

Fig. 2

Fig. 3

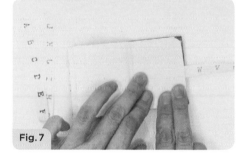

Fig. 4

Fig. 5

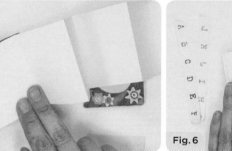

Fig. 6

Fig. 7

3 Decorate the front and back covers any way you desire. Use cookie cutters to cut out flattened pieces of another color of clay. Press them onto the covers. (Fig. 2 & 3)

4 Follow the manufacturer's instructions for baking the clay. Allow the clay to cool.

5 Begin the pages of the book. Set the 18" (45.5 cm) piece of paper in front of you. Make the first fold 2" (5 cm) wide. Then continue folding the sheet back and forth until complete.

6 Drizzle glue around the inside edges of the book's front cover. Place the accordion-folded paper on top. On the inside front cover, draw a 1" (2.5 cm) line of glue that extends from the center to the outer edge. Place one end of a piece of ribbon on top of the line of glue. Then place a 2" × 3" (5 × 7.5 cm) piece of paper on top. The paper will sandwich the ribbon. Repeat step 6 on the back cover. Allow the book to dry while open. (Fig. 4–7)

7 Use the book for writing and sketching. Use the ribbons to tie the book closed.

SUSHI FOR SUPPER

In display cases on the outsides of restaurants in Japan, you'll find realistic looking fake food. These food sculptures are called *sampuru*, which means "sample." Let's create our own Japanese food sculptures with clay sushi!

Tools&
Materials

polymer clay, in several colors, including black and white

rolling pin or jar

garlic press

skewer

ruler or strip of stiff cardboard

Mod Podge

fine green glitter

1 Sushi is often wrapped in nori, or dried seaweed, which is black. Pinch off a piece of black polymer clay the size of a gumball. Roll it into a short snake and flatten it between your fingers. Use the rolling pin to flatten and stretch it. (Fig. 1)

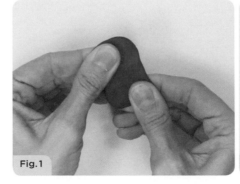

Fig. 1

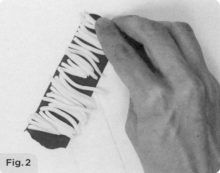

Fig. 2

Fig. 3

Fig. 4

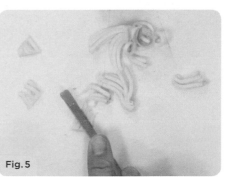
Fig. 5

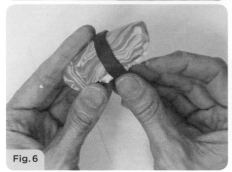
Fig. 6

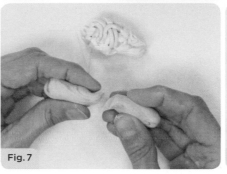
Fig. 7

Fig. 8

2 To create rice, place white polymer clay in the garlic press and squeeze. Place strings of the white clay on top of the nori. (Fig. 2)

3 Some sushi rolls include carrots, cucumber, and avocado. Place orange clay inside the garlic press and squeeze. Add the orange strings to the middle of the sushi. Add green for vegetables and pink for fish. (Fig. 3)

4 Gently roll the sushi. If any clay is sticking out of the roll, trim it off with a ruler edge. (Fig. 4)

5 To make uramaki, create more rice. Attach the rice on the outside of the sushi. (Fig. 5)

6 Nigiri is one type of fresh fish served on rice. We will make two types of nigiri: salmon and shrimp. Create rice and compress it into an oval. Blend orange and white clay to create salmon. Roll the blended colors into a short snake and squeeze it flat. Place it on top of the mound of rice. (Fig. 6)

7 Create another mound of rice as in step 6. To make the shrimp, use a light pink colored clay. Roll it into a snake and fold

it in half. While holding one end, begin to twist it. Flatten the two ends for the tail. Add it to the mound of rice. (Fig. 7)

8 Create chopsticks, wasabi, ginger, and a soy sauce bowl using the methods you've learned.

9 Bake all of the clay sushi pieces according to the manufacturer's directions. Allow the clay to dry.

10 Mix a little Mod Podge with a sprinkle of fine green glitter. Paint it on the nori to give it a little shimmer. (Fig. 8)

GLITTER BUGS

When creating with polymer clay, you'll often end up with a lot of leftover pieces. You might be tempted to throw them away, but don't. You can use them for fun sculptures like these glitter bugs. You can also create these insects without the little gemstones.

Tools & Materials

polymer clay

skewer

small metal-backed gemstones

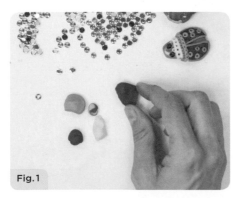

Fig. 1

1 Decide what size bug to make. Roll a piece of clay into a ball that would make a good bug body. Shape it as you like and set it aside. (Fig. 1)

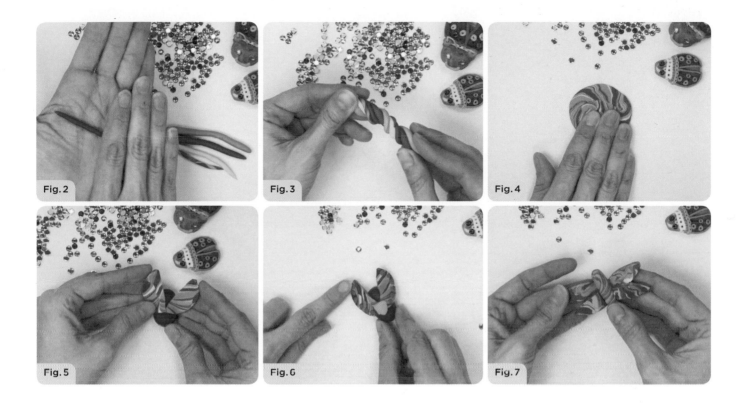

Fig. 2

Fig. 3

Fig. 4

Fig. 5

Fig. 6

Fig. 7

2 Pick about four pieces of scrap clay and roll them into small snakes, all about the same length. (Fig. 2)

3 Twist the snakes, creating a rope of clay. Once twisted, form it into a ball. (Fig. 3)

4 Do this several times until the mix of colors is pleasing. Flatten the clay. Cut it with the skewer into a circle, larger than the bug body. Cut the circle in half. Attach the two pieces to the body as the bug's wings. (Fig. 5)

5 Add details, such as small dots of clay, stripes of color, and parts of the bug's body. Try making other insects like dragonflies and bees. (Fig. 6 & 7)

6 Shape a piece of green clay into a ball. Flatten it and cut it into a leaf shape. Place the bug on the leaf.

7 Press gemstones into the polymer clay.

8 Follow the manufacturer's directions for baking the clay bugs.

LAB 34

MONSTER MAGNETS

Doesn't every refrigerator need a three-eyed monster? How about a mustached Cyclops or a big-eyed, buck-toothed creature? Explore creating a variety of silly monster features that you can change, rearrange, and stick to any metal surface!

Tools & Materials

polymer clay, in a variety of colors

skewer

self-adhesive magnets

scissors

metallic pen or marker

glue

1 Start making an eye by cutting and rolling a piece of clay into a ball the size of a gumball. Flatten the ball. (Fig. 1)

2 Make a smaller ball of clay with another color. Flatten it and place it on top of the first piece to create the iris—the colorful part of the eye.

3 For more color, add tiny pieces of flattened clay on top of the iris. (Fig. 2)

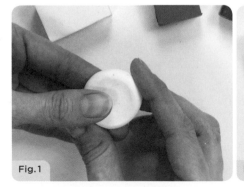

Fig. 1

Fig. 2

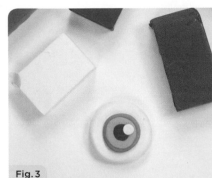
Fig. 3

Fig. 4

Fig. 5

Fig. 6

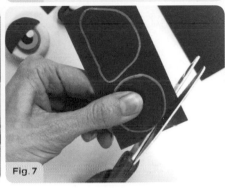
Fig. 7

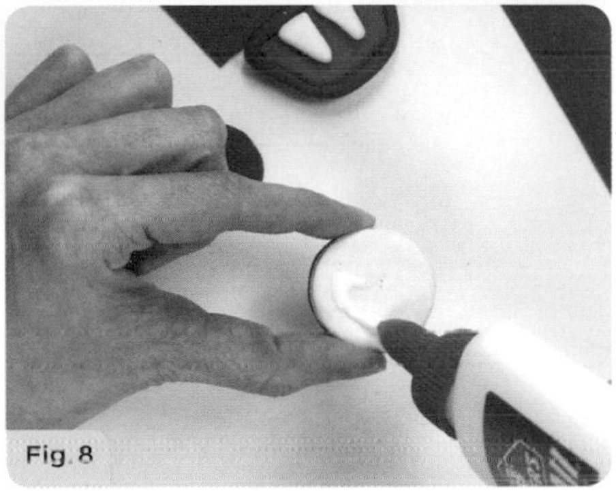

Fig. 8

4 Add a small dot of clay for the pupil in the center of the eye and a white highlight. (Fig. 3)

5 If desired, make another eye, a little different than the first. Or make some variations: Connect two circles to make attached eyes. Add a flattened circle cut in half to create an eyelid. Make some eyelashes! (Fig. 4)

6 Make a mustache by flattening a piece of clay into a shape you like. Add texture with the skewer. You can create a fancy mustache by overlapping two pieces of clay shaped like wings. For a mouth, flatten a large ball of clay. Use the skewer to cut the outer edge of the flattened clay into the shape of a mouth. Flatten, cut out, and add different colors of clay for teeth and a tongue. (Fig. 5)

7 Bake the clay according to the directions on the package. Allow the clay to cool.

8 Trace the creature features onto a piece of magnet and cut out the shape. Attach the features to the magnet by peeling and attaching the sticky back. If you are not using self-adhesive magnets, simply attach the features to the magnet with glue. (Fig. 6–8)

DAY OF THE DEAD HEADS

The Day of the Dead or *el Dia de los Muertos* is a Mexican holiday that is celebrated by many people around the world. During this multi-day holiday, people remember friends and family members who have passed away. But this is not a sad day! There are parades with giant *calaveras,* or handmade skulls, and music in the streets. Create your own fun and funky calavera in this lab.

Tools & Materials

8" (20.5 cm) square of aluminum foil

one block of white polymer clay per head

polymer clay, in a variety of colors, including black

small metal backed gems (optional)

gold acrylic paint (optional)

paintbrushes

1 Crumple the foil into an oval-shaped ball about the size of a golf ball. (Fig. 1)

2 Warm a block of white polymer clay between your hands and squeeze it to soften it. Flatten the clay on your work surface. (Fig. 2)

Fig. 1

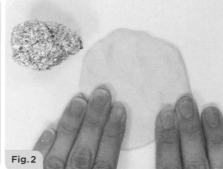

Fig. 2

Fig. 3

Fig. 4

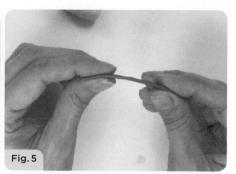

Fig. 5

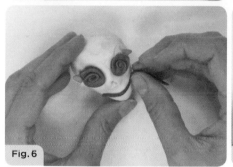

Fig. 6

Fig. 7

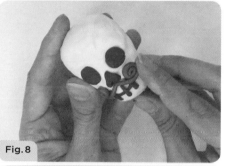

Fig. 8

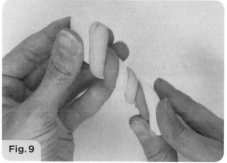

Fig. 9

3 Fold the clay over the foil ball, flattening any lumps. Use small pieces of clay to fill in any exposed spots. (Fig. 3)

4 Gently press eye sockets into the clay head with your fingers. Roll small pieces of black clay and place them into the sockets. (Fig. 4)

5 To make flowers, roll a small piece of clay into a snake. Flatten it between your fingers. Starting at one end, roll the clay. Pinch it on one end so that it resembles a rose.

6 Use a skinny snake of black clay for the mouth. Add smaller pieces of clay along the mouth for the teeth. Shape a clay heart and place it upside down on the skull for the nose. (Fig. 5-7)

7 Get creative! Add a mustache, a floral crown, glasses, or a hat to your dead heads. (Fig. 8)

8 To create a colorful background, roll three colors of clay snakes and twist them together. Form them into a ball, and then roll them into a snake again. Repeat so that the colors in the clay swirl. (Fig. 9)

9 Flatten the piece of clay and add it to the back of the skull's head.

10 Follow the manufacturer's baking instructions. Allow the clay to cool and decorate it with gems and/or paint.

BACKPACK CHARMS

Charms give you a fun way to showcase your interests—your favorite food, sport, hobby, or anything else. In this lab, you'll use the sculpting skills you've learned in previous creations to make unique charms to add to your backpack or a necklace or bracelet. You'll need a variety of colors of polymer clay to create these mini-masterpieces. Everyone's choices will be different for this lab, so use your imagination to create your charm.

Tools & Materials

pencil

paper

variety pack of polymer clay

scissors

skewer

jump rings

1 Jot down your favorite foods, hobbies, and other things. Sketch a few designs before creating. My favorite thing is art, so I decided to sculpt a paint palette.

2 Blend together two colors to create the wood for the palette. When the colors have the appearance of wood grain, flatten it between your fingers. (Fig. 1)

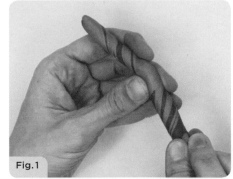

Fig. 1

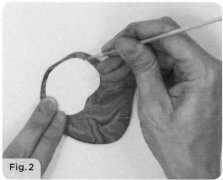

Fig. 2

Fig. 3

Fig. 4

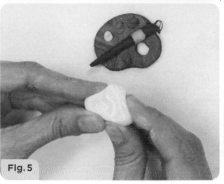

Fig. 5

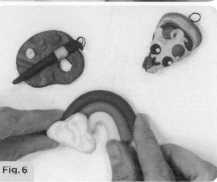

Fig. 6

3 On a piece of paper, draw a small palette shape about the size of a quarter and cut it out. Place the paper template on the flattened clay and trace around it with the skewer. (Fig. 2)

4 To make the paintbrush, roll a tiny snake of clay about 1" (2.5 cm) long. Add a little bit of black to the top for the brush and a bit of silver between the brush and the handle. Gently press the brush onto the palette. (Fig. 3)

5 Add little dollops of clay in different colors around the edge of the palette as paint.

6 Before baking, press a jump ring into the clay. This will be where the charm clips are added.

7 Follow the manufacturer's directions to bake your charms. Allow the clay to cool before handling or wearing them.

TIP: Go back through the labs in this book. Look for the directions for creating donuts, fortune cookies, pizza, cupcakes, rainbows, and other fun items. Sculpt these on a miniature scale and add the jump ring before baking. (Fig. 4-6)

GAME PIECES AND DICE FOR YOUR OWN GAME

A board game is fun to play. But it's even more fun when you create your very own! Begin by thinking of a theme for your game: aliens, monsters, robots, snack foods, zoo animals—you name it. Then think of a clever environment for your characters: a different planet, a refrigerator, or a wild safari. You'll be putting these fun ideas of yours together to create a game for you to play with family and friends!

Tools & Materials

variety pack of polymer clay

skewer

9" × 12" (23 × 30.5 cm) poster board

watercolor paint

water cup

paintbrushes

permanent markers

10 pieces of 1"× 2" (2.5 × 5 cm) paper

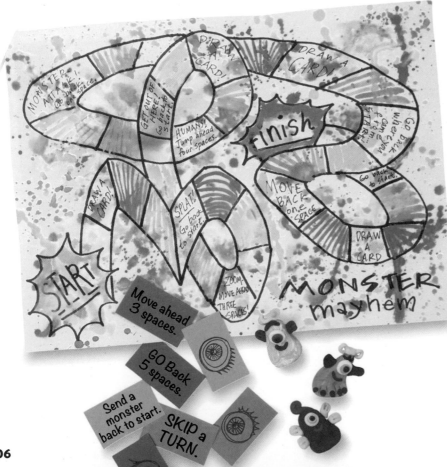

1 Decide on a theme and create three to six game pieces. Start with pieces of clay no bigger than a gumball. Roll the clay into a ball. Press it firmly onto a table so that it has a flat base. (Fig. 1)

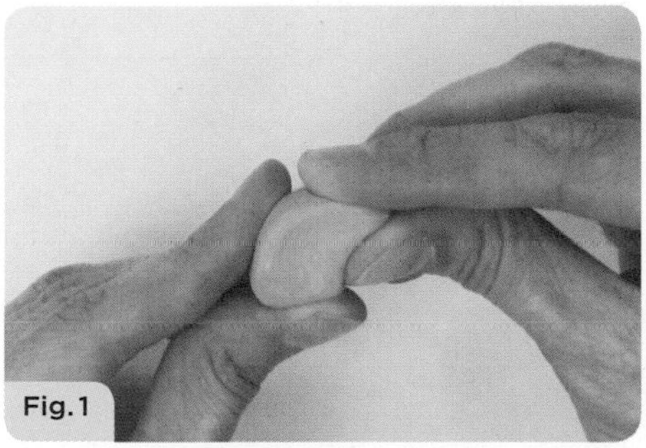

Fig. 1

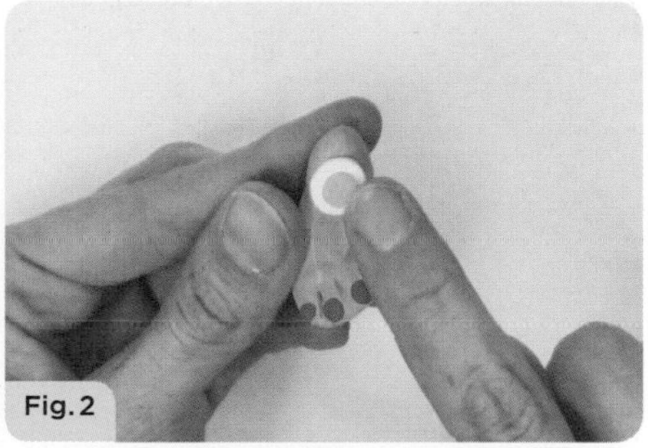

Fig. 2

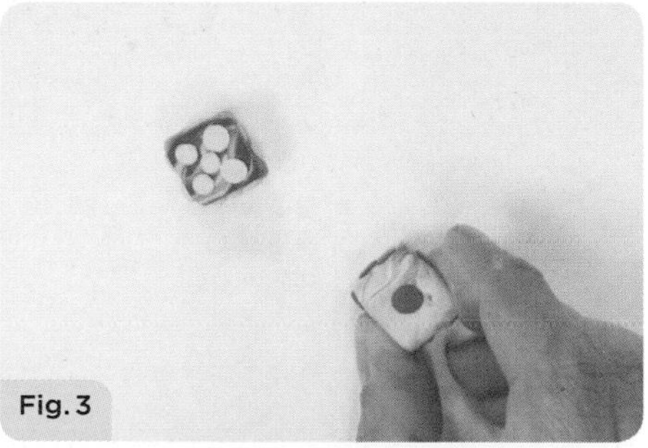

Fig. 3

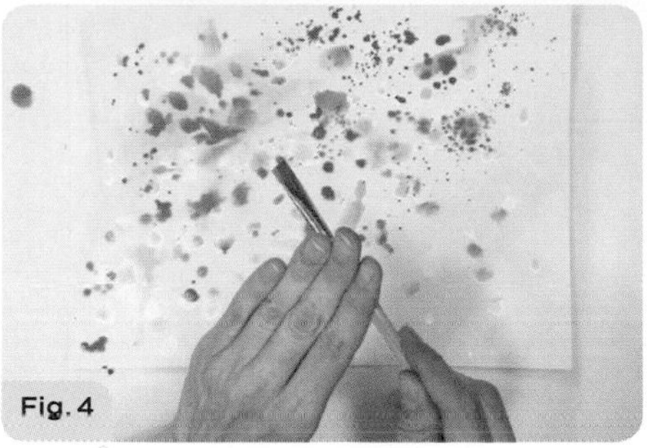

Fig. 4

Fig. 5

Fig. 6

2 Add features to the pieces. If they are monsters, add eyes, mouths, and silly details. For animals, add the characteristics that make them unique. (Fig. 2)

3 To create the dice, use a piece of clay the size of a gumball. Roll it into a ball and then shape it into a cube between your fingers. (Fig. 3)

4 With small pieces of clay in a contrasting color, add dots to the dice. Each side of the dice should have a different number of dots from one to six.

5 Follow the manufacturer's directions to bake the game pieces and the dice. Allow the clay to cool.

6 Design the game board any way you want. For a splatter paint board, paint the entire surface with water. Then, using watercolors, dip the brush into the paint and gently tap the back of the brush to splatter the paint. Allow it to dry completely. (Fig. 4)

7 Using a permanent marker, draw a "start" spot for the game. Make this spot big enough for all the pieces to fit into. (Fig. 5)

8 Draw a line for the path of the game. Draw another line about 1" (2.5 cm) from the first one to create parallel lines. Divide the path into spaces with short lines. It will resemble a sidewalk.

9 Write silly directions in these spaces such as "go back to start" or "take three steps forward." (Fig. 6)

10 Create a small deck of draw cards with more directions on them. Don't forget to add a couple of spaces that state "draw a card." Give the game a name! Play the game!

LET YOUR LIGHT SHINE NIGHTLIGHT

Create your own nightlight using some of the polymer clay left over from other creations. Never throw away your scraps of polymer clay because you can always use it for fun projects like this one! Customizing your own nightlight will add a little bit of bright to your night.

Tools & Materials

polymer clay, in various colors

skewer

inexpensive nightlight

small metal polymer stamps

glue

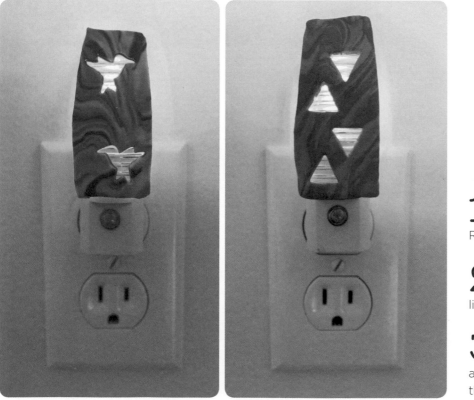

1 Pinch off three gumball-sized pieces of different colors clay. Roll each into a snake.

2 Hold the snakes at one end and twist them until they look like a candy cane. (Fig. 1)

3 Squash the twisted cane and form it into a ball. Roll it into a long snake and twist it again so that the colors swirl. (Fig. 2)

Fig. 1

Fig. 2

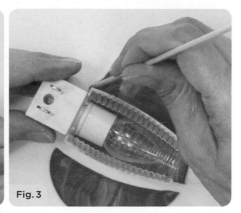

Fig. 3

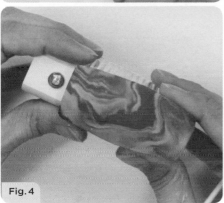

Fig. 4

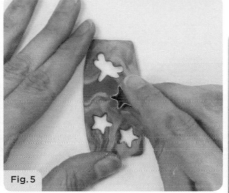

Fig. 5

4 Flatten the clay on your work surface. Place the nightlight on top. Trace around the edge of the nightlight with the skewer to cut out the shape. Set the nightlight aside. (Fig. 3 & 4)

5 Create a design in the clay with the metal clay stamps. (Fig. 5)

6 Bake the clay according to manufacturer's instructions. Allow it to cool.

7 Use glue to adhere the design to the night light. Plug it in!

FUNKY FAUX-SAIC

Mosaics are works of art created from small pieces of glass, stone, or clay. Usually, the bits and bobs are attached to a surface with glue, and grout is added to fill in the in between spaces. Our mosaic—on a door sign or terra cotta pot—is created differently. That's why ours is a *faux* or fake mosaic!

Tools & Materials

wood or terra cotta
item, such as
wooden door sign
or terra cotta pot

polymer clay

skewer

scissors

metal polymer stamps
(optional)

large baking sheet

glue

paintbrushes

Mod Podge (optional)

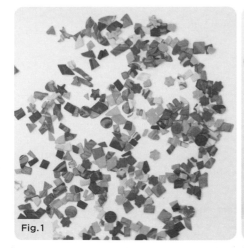
Fig. 1

Fig. 2

Fig. 3

Fig. 4

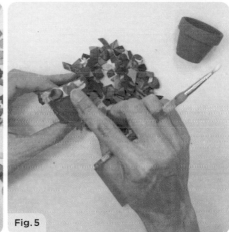
Fig. 5

1 Choose something to cover with faux-saic. Wood surfaces and terra cotta pottery work well.

2 Prepare the fake mosaic tiles by flattening the polymer clay and cutting it into strips with the skewer. (Fig. 1)

3 Use scissors or polymer stamps to cut the clay into small shapes.

4 Place the tiles on a large baking sheet and spread them out. If some are touching, it's fine. Follow the manufacturer's instructions to bake the clay tiles. Allow the clay to cool. Gently break apart any tiles that have stuck together.

5 Plan a design for the surface you want to cover. Brush glue on small portions of the surface. (Fig. 2 & 3)

6 Arrange the tiles in place on the glued sections, leaving just a little bit of space in between. Repeat, brushing on glue and arranging tiles on top. (Fig. 4 & 5)

7 Once all the tiles are in place, allow the glue to dry overnight.

8 To ensure that the tiles will stay in place, add a layer of Mod Podge over the entire surface.

DESKTOP DINOS

Many sculptures have something called an *armature* underneath the outer shape. An armature functions like the skeleton that supports the shape. For your Desktop Dino, you will create an armature from aluminum foil.

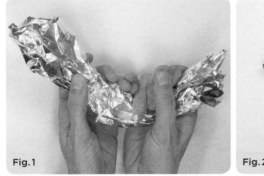

Fig. 1

Fig. 2

1 Gently crumple the foil until it resembles a snake. Bend it into a *U* shape. Pinch one end for the dinosaur's tail. (Fig. 1)

2 The other end of the foil will be the dinosaur's head. To create an armature that will have an open mouth, gently tear the foil about 1" (2.5 cm). Crumple the top and bottom of the torn piece until it resembles the open mouth of a dinosaur.

3 Choose any color clay for the dinosaur. To blend two colors, roll them both into snakes and twist one around the other. Form the twist into a ball. Roll the ball into a snake. Continue twisting and rolling until the clay has created a swirled pattern or has blended completely. (Fig. 2)

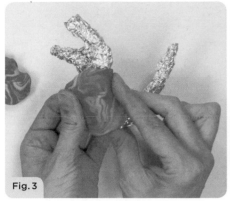

Fig. 3

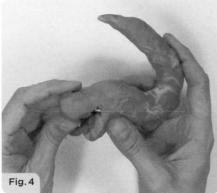

Fig. 4

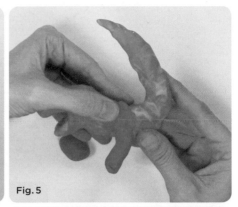

Fig. 5

4 Pinch off pieces of the clay and squish them into thin pieces for the dinosaur's skin. Drape the pieces over the armature. Gently press them into place (Fig. 3)

5 Continue flattening the clay and adding it to the aluminum until the entire armature is covered. (Fig. 4)

6 To create the short front legs of a Tyrannosaurus Rex, roll two small pieces of clay and add them on either side of the dinosaur's body. (Fig. 5)

7 To create the dinosaur's back legs, roll longer, thicker pieces and add them to the sides. Bend the feet so that the dinosaur can stand. (Fig. 6)

8 Create a scaly texture by rolling small balls of clay and pressing them onto the dinosaur's skin. Add eyes and teeth with small pieces of clay.

9 Before baking, be certain that the dinosaur can stand. If it falls over, adjust the head and legs until it balances.

10 Follow the manufacturer's directions to bake the clay, with the aluminum inside. Allow the clay to cool.

11 Paint some details onto your dinosaur and allow to dry. Add gloss with Mod Podge or mix fine glitter with Mod Podge before brushing it on.

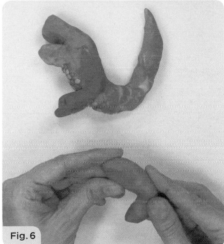

Fig. 6

MAKING YOUR OWN CLAY

~~~~~

In the following labs, you get

to be a chef, a scientist, and an artist as you mix and create with your own clay. Most of the clay recipes call for a handful of basic household ingredients. None of them require cooking, and only a few will need some time in an oven on low heat. When using food coloring to color your homemade clay, be certain to cover your work space and wear gloves so you don't stain your hands.

Most of all, have fun mixing up your batches of clay!

SIMPLE NO-COOK CLAY

The best thing about homemade clay is making it! Because we'll be using cooking supplies, it's best to create this clay in the kitchen for easy cleanup. This clay recipe is simple and requires very few ingredients. You can also reuse this clay by keeping it in an airtight zipper-lock bag. If the clay becomes dry while you're working, simply add more water. If you create something you'd like to keep, leave it out to air-dry.

Tools & Materials

large mixing bowl

measuring cups

2 cups (250 g) all-purpose flour

¾ cup (216 g) salt

¾ cup (175 ml) warm water

zipper-lock bag

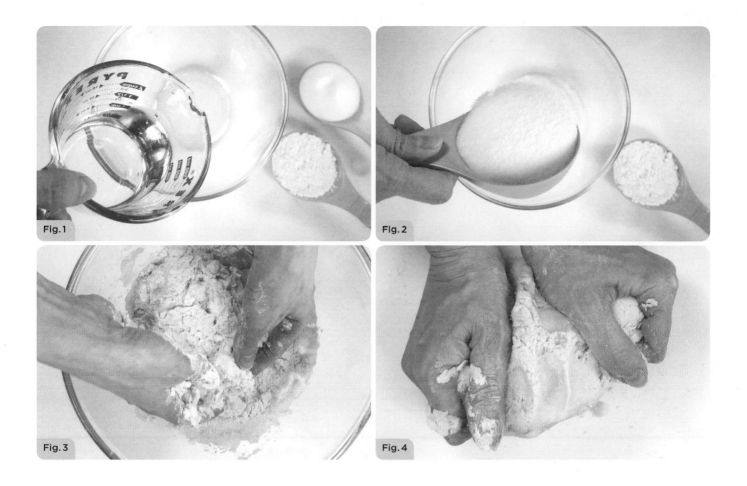

Fig. 1

Fig. 2

Fig. 3

Fig. 4

1 In the mixing bowl, measure and add all three ingredients. (Fig. 1 & 2)

2 Use your hands to knead or squeeze the ingredients together. Do this for two to three minutes or until all of the ingredients combine like a ball of dough. (If it's too hard to knead it all at once, split the ball of dough in half and continue to knead.) (Fig. 3 & 4)

3 Once the ball of clay is smooth, it is time to create! To combine pieces of clay, simply apply water as if it were glue. To save your creation, set it out to dry overnight. You can store unused clay in an airtight zipper-lock bag to be used again in the future.

LAB 42

STAMPED CLAY ORNAMENTS

Making ornaments is a fun and easy way to create small gifts and explore the textures of rubber stamps. Once these ornaments are dry, they can be painted and strung up with colorful ribbon or twine.

Tools & Materials

Simple No-Cook Clay
(Lab 41,
pages 116–117)

rubber stamps

skewer

watercolor paint

paintbrushes

ribbon or twine

Fig. 1

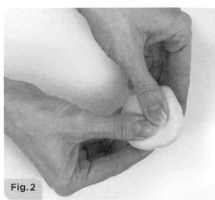

Fig. 2

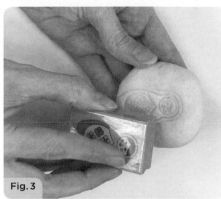

Fig. 3

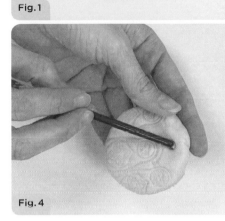

Fig. 4

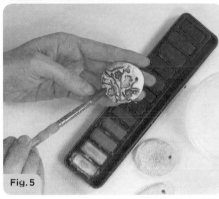

Fig. 5

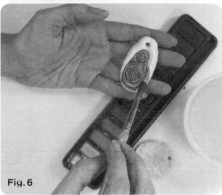

Fig. 6

1 Pinch off a piece of clay about the size of a gumball. Roll it into a smooth ball. Flatten the ball between the palms of your hands. (Fig. 1 & 2)

2 Press a stamp into the flattened clay. Stamps that have a deep design work best. Stamps with small fine details do not always work well with this clay, but it's fun to experiment.

3 If you are not pleased with the stamped design, roll it up and try it again. If the clay begins to crack, rub in a little bit of water. (Fig. 3)

4 Poke a hole in the top of the ornament with the skewer. (Fig. 4)

5 Allow the ornament to dry overnight. Turn it over after several hours to ensure that both sides dry.

6 Paint the ornaments with watercolor. Allow the paint to dry. (Fig. 5 & 6)

7 String a ribbon or twine through the hole for hanging.

SCENTED CLAY ACORNS

Here is a perfect fall project. You won't believe how wonderful these acorns smell!

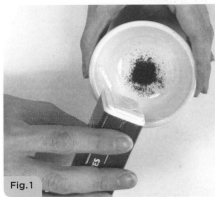

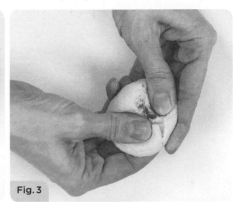

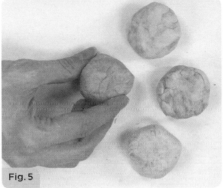

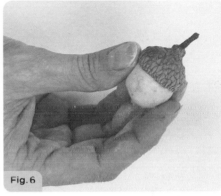

1 Divide the clay into Ping-Pong ball-size pieces.

2 Sprinkle about ¼ teaspoon of spice into the bowl. Roll each of the clay balls around in the bowl. (Fig. 1 & 2)

3 Work the clay by smashing it between your hands and rolling it into a ball again. (Fig. 3)

4 For a stronger scent, sprinkle more spice into the bowl and repeat. If too much spice is added, it can cause the clay to dry out. This can be remedied by adding just a touch of water to the clay. (Fig. 4 & 5)

5 Set out the acorn tops. Press a scented ball of clay inside each acorn top. Allow them to dry overnight. (Fig. 6)

6 To hang the scented acorns, glue a length of string to the tops and allow it to dry.

MAKE YOUR OWN PLAY DOUGH

This recipe for play dough smells delicious because of the Kool Aid. However, because it is made with salt, you won't want to taste it! If you keep this clay in resealable containers, you can play with it again and again. However, in Lab 45, you'll see how you can make a colorful keepsake with your Kool Aid play dough.

Tools & Materials

2½ cups (313 g) all-purpose flour

½ cup (144 g) salt

1 tablespoon (19 g) cream of tartar

large bowl

small bowls (the same number as you have Kool-Aid packets)

variety of unsweetened Kool-Aid packets

1 cup (235 ml) water

spoon

wax paper

3 resealable containers

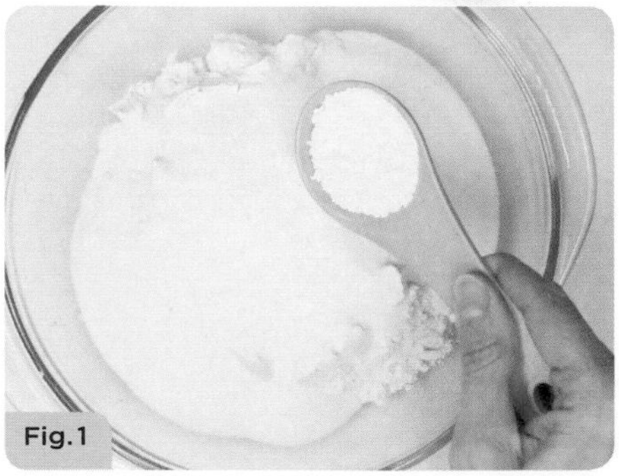

Fig. 1

1 Mix the flour, salt, and cream of tartar together in a large bowl. (Fig. 1)

2 Divide the flour mixture evenly among the smaller bowls. No measurement is needed, simply eyeball the amount to see whether it looks even.

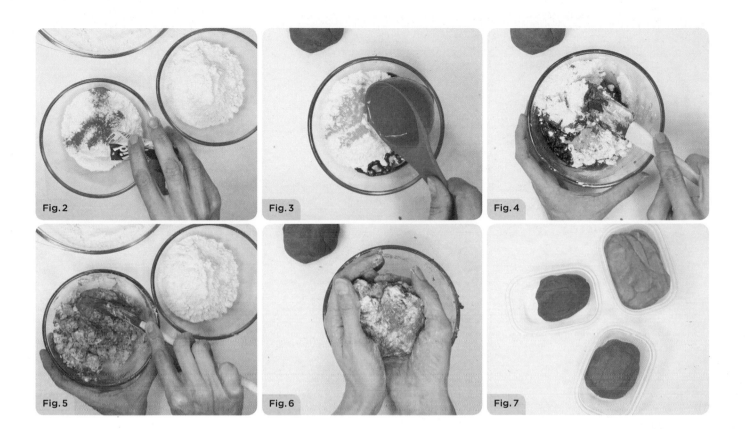

Fig. 2

Fig. 3

Fig. 4

Fig. 5

Fig. 6

Fig. 7

3 Pour a different color Kool-Aid packet into each of the flour mixtures. (Fig. 2)

4 Slowly pour water into the bowl. (Fig. 3)

5 Mix with a spoon. The mixture should be clumpy and slightly sticky. It should not crumble. If it does, add a small amount of water. (Fig. 4 & 5)

6 Dump the mixture from one bowl onto the wax paper. Use your hands to knead the clay until the color is evenly blended and there are no lumps in the clay. (Fig. 6)

7 Follow these steps for the different colors of Kool Aid.

8 Store Kool-Aid play dough in separate resealable containers for future use. (Fig. 7)

CLAY ICE POPS

When you grow tired of using your play dough, you can create these fun ice pop sculptures! They look so real that you might even be able to fool your friends into thinking they're edible. Adding clear glitter really gives the ice pops a frosty appearance.

Tools & Materials

Play Dough,
in several colors
(Lab 44,
pages 122–123)

ice pop sticks

wax paper

Mod Podge

paintbrushes

clear glitter

1 Follow the recipe for making Play Dough in Lab 44. Pick two different colors of the Play Dough to swirl together for one ice pop. Each of the two pieces should be about the size of a Ping-Pong ball.

2 Roll each piece of play dough into a long snake. They should be the same length. (Fig. 1)

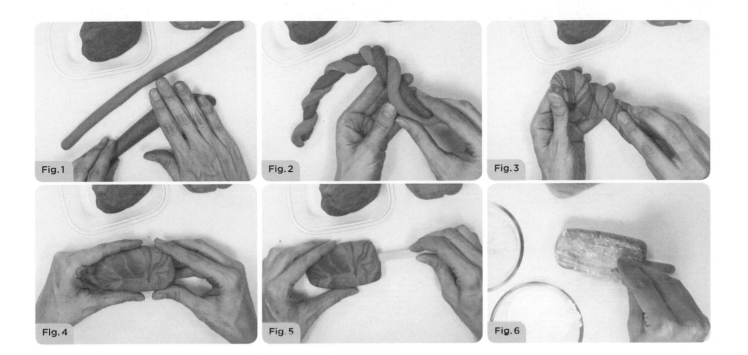

Fig. 1

Fig. 2

Fig. 3

Fig. 4

Fig. 5

Fig. 6

3 Put the two snakes next to each other. With one hand, hold them together at the top. With the other hand, begin twisting the two snakes together. The twist should look a little like a candy cane. (Fig. 2)

4 Shape the twist into a ball, and then roll it into a snake again. The two doughs should be starting to mix and swirl together. To blend more, pinch the snake at the top and twist with the other hand as in step 3. (Fig. 3)

5 Form the clay into a ball again and then roll it into a short snake. Gently pressing it onto your work surface, shape the clay to resemble an ice pop shape. (Fig. 4)

6 Slide an ice pop stick into the bottom of the dough. (Fig. 5)

7 Allow the clay to dry on waxed paper overnight. Turn the ice pop over every so often so that it dries evenly.

8 To add some icy sparkle, paint a coat of Mod Podge onto one side of the ice pop. Sprinkle with clear glitter. (Fig. 6)

9 Allow the Mod Podge and glitter to dry for a few hours before repeating step 8 on the back and sides.

JURASSIC FOSSILS WITH SAND CLAY

The Jurassic period was a time when dinosaurs roamed the Earth. In this lab, you will use sand to create your own clay, and you'll also be able to create dinosaur fossils! You and your friends can have fun burying and excavating these fossils just like paleontologists.

1 In a large bowl, stir the sand, flour, and salt together with the spoon. (Fig. 1)

2 While stirring, slowly add the water. When the clay can no longer be mixed with the spoon, use your hands. (Fig. 2)

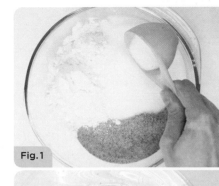

Fig. 1

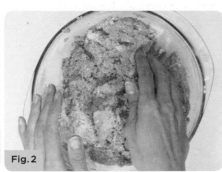

Fig. 2

Fig. 3

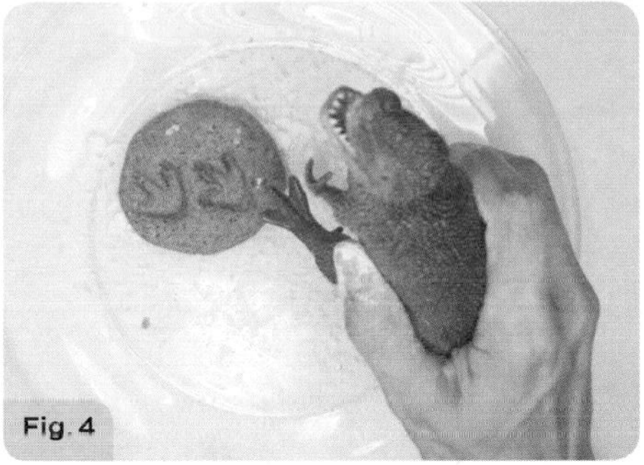

Fig. 4

Fig. 5

Fig. 6

3 Split the clay into small pieces about the size of a golf ball.

4 For a bit of sparkle, press the clay into a container of glitter and work it into the clay. (Fig. 3)

5 Place wax paper on a plate and cover it with a sprinkle of flour. Flatten the clay onto the paper.

6 Use plastic toys such as dinosaurs and cars. Press the dinosaur feet firmly into the clay. Try driving a toy car through the clay. (Fig. 4–6)

7 If it's a sunny day, place the plate in the sun to dry. Flip the clay pieces over every couple of hours. The clay can also be dried indoors for a couple of days.

8 Once the clay is dry, use brown and black watercolor to paint it. Paint the indentations one color and the rest of the clay a different color. This will make the fossils more visible. (Fig. 7)

9 Take the fossils outside and bury them. Have fun excavating your dinosaur fossils!

Fig. 7

GLITTER CLAY BEADS

This lab uses the recipe from Lab 41, but this time, you'll add color and sparkle to your clay. You'll also learn how to mix the three primary colors—red, yellow, and blue—to create the secondary colors—orange, green, and purple. This recipe makes a lot of clay. Store the extra in airtight zipper-lock bags.

2 Divide the clay into three equal parts. Place the clay into individual zipper-lock bags. Add three or four drops of food coloring to each to make one red, one yellow, and one blue. (Fig. 1)

3 Squeeze a bag until the food coloring and the clay are evenly mixed. If the color is too light, add more food coloring and continue squeezing bag. (Fig. 2)

4 Sprinkle in glitter the same color as the clay. Squeeze the bag until eveything is well mixed. Remove it from the bags.

1 Make the Simple No-Cook Clay recipe from Lab 41 (pages 116–117). Knead the clay with your hands until it's smooth.

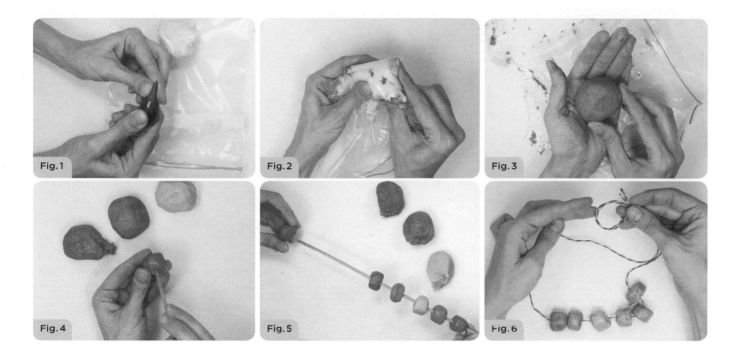

Fig. 1

Fig. 2

Fig. 3

Fig. 4

Fig. 5

Fig. 6

5 The food coloring used on the clay may stain your hands. Wear disposable gloves before handling the clay. Roll each color of clay into a ball. (Fig. 3)

6 To make the beads for a rainbow necklace, pinch off a piece of red clay the size of a gumball. Roll into a ball. Slowly slide it onto the pointed end of a skewer. (Fig. 4)

7 To create orange, pinch off a piece of yellow clay and a smaller piece of red. Roll the two colors between your hands until orange is created. Slide it onto the skewer.

8 To create green, use yellow and blue. Use a little more yellow than blue to create green.

9 To create purple, use equal parts red and blue.

10 Slide all of the beads onto the skewer in rainbow order: red, orange, yellow, green, blue, and purple. Allow the beads to dry overnight. (Fig. 5)

11 Cut a piece of string, yarn, or twine so that it is about 24" (61 cm) long.

12 Slide the beads onto the string in rainbow order. Use a double knot to tie the ends of the string. Enjoy wearing your necklace. (Fig. 6)

MAKE YOUR OWN SILLY PUTTY

Silly Putty is not clay that you can sculpt. Instead, it is great for working up those hand muscles by squeezing and playing with it. But the best part about this Silly Putty is making it. It is messy, sticky fun!

Tools & Materials

4 oz (120 ml) bottle of Elmer's Glue All

mixing bowl

measuring cup

food coloring

spoon

½ cup (120 ml) Sta Flo concentrated liquid starch

wax paper

zipper-lock bag

Fig. 1

Fig. 2

Fig. 3

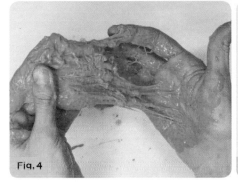

Fig. 4

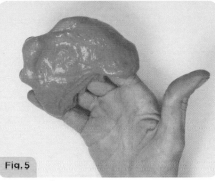

Fig. 5

Fig. 6

1 Pour the entire contents of the bottle of glue into the bowl. Add one or two drops of food coloring and stir. (Fig. 1 & 2)

2 Pour the liquid starch into the bowl. Let the glue, starch, and food coloring sit in the bowl for five minutes. (Fig. 3)

3 Cover your work surface with wax paper. Dump the mixture onto the wax paper.

4 Pull and squeeze the Silly Putty for five to ten minutes. At first it will be very sticky! Keep pulling, squeezing, and rolling it into a ball until it is no longer so tacky. (Fig. 4-6)

5 Once the Silly Putty is mixed thoroughly, it can bounce, and it can even pull prints from the newspaper.

6 Store your Silly Putty in an airtight zipper-lock bag to play with later.

SALT DOUGH RECIPE AND ROSE SCULPTURE

This recipe is similar to the one in Lab 41, but the artwork you make from it will be baked. This will harden the clay and allow you to paint it right away. To make less clay, divide all of the ingredients in half.

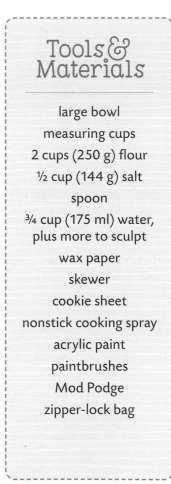

Tools & Materials

large bowl
measuring cups
2 cups (250 g) flour
½ cup (144 g) salt
spoon
¾ cup (175 ml) water,
plus more to sculpt
wax paper
skewer
cookie sheet
nonstick cooking spray
acrylic paint
paintbrushes
Mod Podge
zipper-lock bag

1 In a large bowl, mix together the flour and salt with the spoon.

2 Slowly add the water and mix it with the spoon. When you can no longer mix it with the spoon, knead the dough with your hands. The dough will have a lumpy texture. (Fig. 1)

3 Cover your work surface with wax paper. Pinch off a piece of dough the size of a large gumball. Roll into a ball. Flatten it between your fingers.

4 To create the center of the rose, start by rolling the edge of the clay inward. Continue rolling until you reach the other side. (Fig. 2)

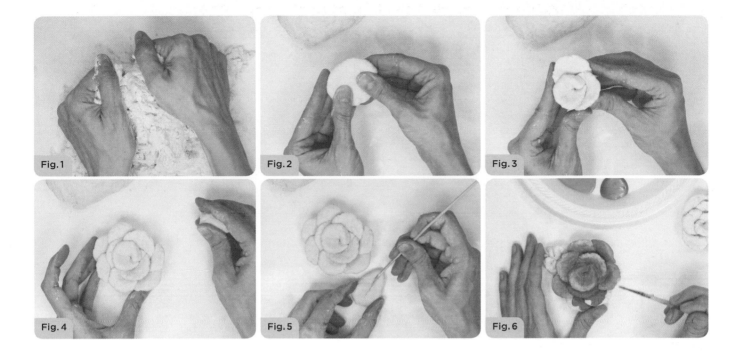

Fig. 1　Fig. 2　Fig. 3
Fig. 4　Fig. 5　Fig. 6

5 To add petals to the rose, pinch off another piece of clay, roll it into a ball, and flatten it. With your finger, add a couple of drops of water to the flattened clay and add it to the outside of the rose center. The water will act like glue. (Fig. 3)

6 Continue rolling, flattening, and adding clay circles with a drop of water to the outside of the rose until it is the size that you want. Press it gently onto the waxed paper. This will create a flat bottom so the rose can stand. (Fig. 4)

7 Pinch a piece of clay and shape it into a leaf. Use the point of the skewer to add veins to the leaf. Add a drop of water to the leaf and stick it to the outside of the rose. (Fig. 5)

8 Preheat the oven to 250°F (120°C, or gas mark ½). Spray the cookie sheet with nonstick cooking spray. Place the rose on the cookie sheet and bake for 25 to 30 minutes. Allow it to cool.

9 To create a rose that looks more three dimensional, paint the rose one color. Then lightly brush white over the top edges of the rose petals. This will create a tint or a lighter version of the rose color. Allow the paint to dry. (Fig. 6)

10 Seal the rose's surface with Mod Podge.

11 Store any extra clay in the zipper-lock bag for later use. It will keep for up to three days if refrigerated.

LAB 50

SALT DOUGH BIRD SCULPTURE

These fun birds make great wall hangings. With their silly expressions and vibrant colors, they are sure to brighten up your day. The same dough used in Lab 49 is used in this lab. You can also create bird sculptures with air-dry clay from a craft store.

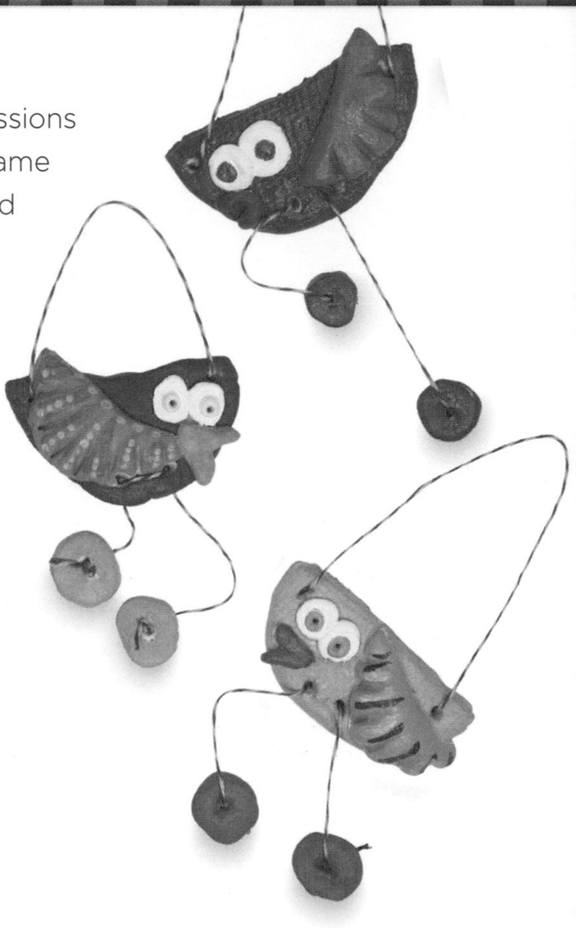

Tools & Materials

- Salt Dough Recipe (Lab 49, pages 132–133)
- textured fabric, such as burlap or lace
- wax paper
- skewer
- small dish of water
- cookie sheet
- nonstick cooking spray
- acrylic paint
- paintbrushes
- Mod Podge
- string, yarn, or twine
- glue

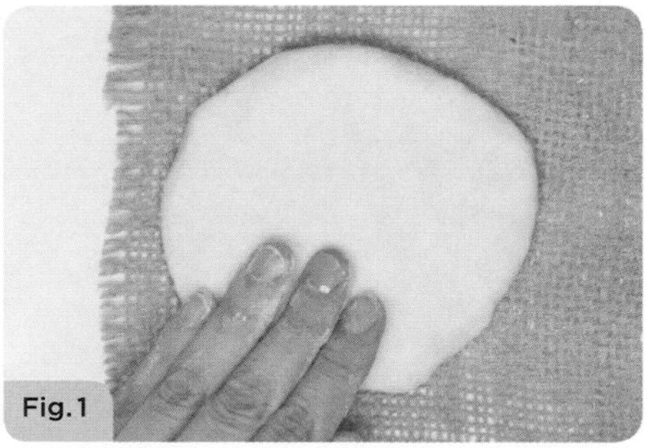

Fig. 1

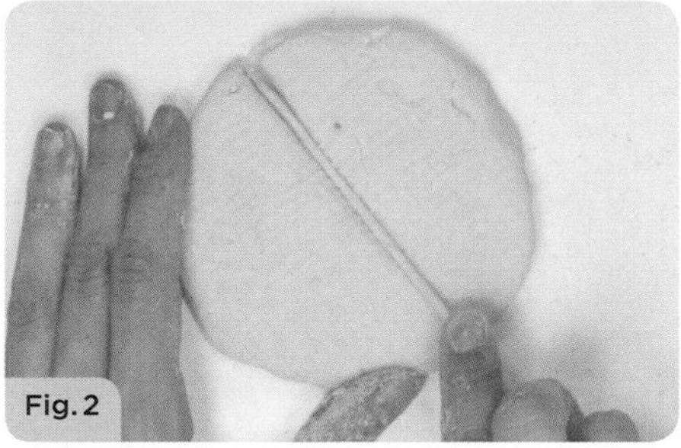

Fig. 2

1 Make the Salt Dough Recipe from Lab 49 (pages 132–133).

2 Use your hands to roll a piece the size of a small orange. Press the clay onto the textured fabric. (Fig. 1)

3 Peel the clay off the fabric slowly. Place it on a sheet of wax paper.

4 Cut the circle of dough in half with the skewer. One half will be the bird's body. The other half is extra clay. (Fig. 2)

Fig. 3

Fig. 4

Fig. 5

Fig. 6

Fig. 7

Fig. 8

5 From the extra clay, pinch off two small pieces for the bird's eyes. Put a dab of water on the back of the eyes to act as glue. Press smaller pieces of clay on top of the circles for the pupils.

6 From the extra clay, pinch off a peanut-sized piece. Roll it into a small snake. Bend the snake in half and place it below the eyes for the beak. (Fig. 3)

7 To create a wing with a small ball of clay, repeat steps 2, 3, and 4. Use half a circle for the wing. (Fig. 4)

8 Poke two holes at the bottom of the bird. Be certain the holes are not too close to each other, nor too close to the bottom edge. Poke two holes at the top of the bird, one at each end. (Fig. 5)

9 For feet, roll two gumball-size pieces of clay. Poke a hole through the balls with the skewer. (Fig. 6)

10 Preheat the oven to 250°F (120°C, or gas mark ½). Spray a cookie sheet with nonstick cooking spray. Bake the birds and beads for 25 to 30 minutes and allow to cool.

11 Paint the bird and beads to decorate. Allow the paint to dry. Add a coat of Mod Podge. (Fig. 7)

12 To assemble the bird, cut two lengths of string about 8" (20.5 cm) long. For the feet, thread the string through the two holes at the bottom of the bird. Thread the two beads for feet. Tie a double knot to secure the beads. (Fig. 8)

13 Thread the string through the front top holes for a hanger—knot the ends. Secure all knots with a drop of glue.

SALT DOUGH TEXTURE FISH

Using the recipe from Lab 49, create these expressive clay fish. They're simple and fun to make. They would also make decorations and gifts for someone who loves to fish!

Tools & Materials

Salt Dough Recipe
(Lab 49,
pages 132–133)

textured fabric, such as burlap or lace

wax paper

small dish of water

skewer

cookie sheet

nonstick cooking spray

acrylic paint

paintbrushes

Mod Podge

1 Make the Salt Dough Recipe from Lab 49 (pages 132–133).

2 When you've mixed the dough, pinch off and roll a piece the size of a small orange. Press it onto the textured fabric.

3 Peel the clay off of the fabric slowly. Place it on a piece of wax paper. (Fig. 1)

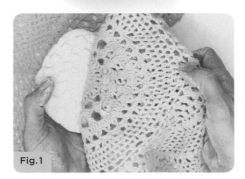

Fig.1

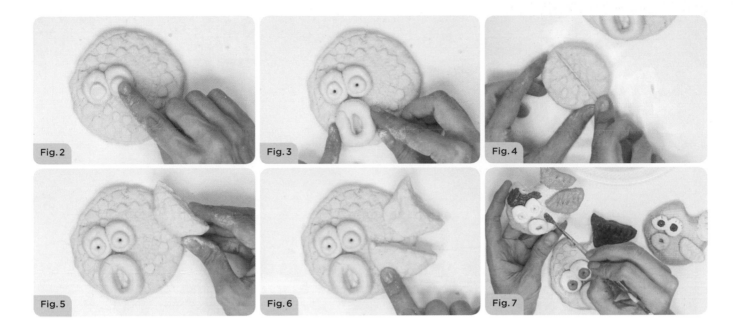

Fig. 2

Fig. 3

Fig. 4

Fig. 5

Fig. 6

Fig. 7

4 Create eyes for the fish by rolling two balls of clay the size of a gumball. Flatten them. Add a little water to the back of the flattened clay with your fingers. Press the eyes next to each other on one side of the clay circle.

5 For the pupils, roll smaller pieces of clay. Add a little water to the back. Place these on the eyes. (Fig. 2)

6 To make the mouth, roll a gumball-size piece of clay into a snake. Shape the snake into a circle. Place it under the eyes. (Fig. 3)

7 To make the tail and fin, roll a Ping-Pong ball–size piece of clay into a ball. Flatten it into a circle on a piece of fabric. Use the skewer to cut it in half. (Fig. 4)

8 Add one half of the circle to the back of the fish for the tail. Add the other half in between the fish face and the tail. This will be the fin. (Fig. 5 & 6)

9 Cut a small piece of clay into a *U* shape. Press it into place at the top of the fish's head.

10 Preheat the oven to 250°F (120°C, or gas mark ½). Spray the cookie sheet with nonstick cooking spray. Place the fish on the cookie sheet and bake for 25 to 30 minutes. Once it's out of the oven, allow it to cool before painting.

11 Use acrylic paint to decorate your fish. Allow the paint to dry. Seal and protect your fish with Mod Podge. (Fig. 7)

LAB 52 — CANDY CLAY

This is the only clay in this book that you can actually eat! It looks and feels like many of the other clays in this book. Look at the other labs for ideas on what to sculpt. Or use cookie cutters to create decorations to add to sweet treats such as cupcakes and cookies. You'll have a blast creating an edible sculpture.

1 Empty the entire package of Candy Melts into the bowl. (Fig. 1)

Fig. 1

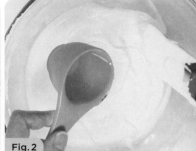
Fig. 2

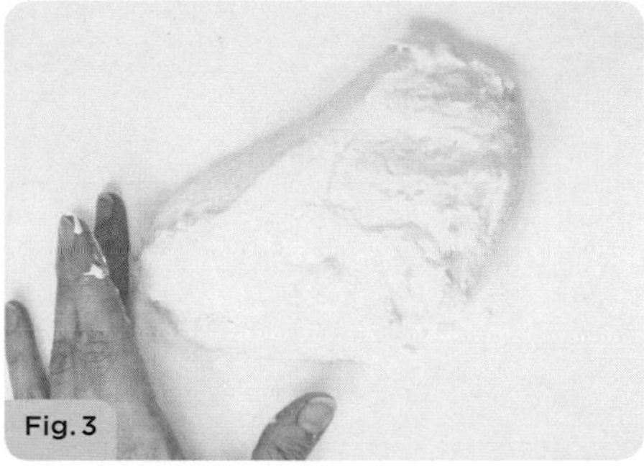

Fig. 3

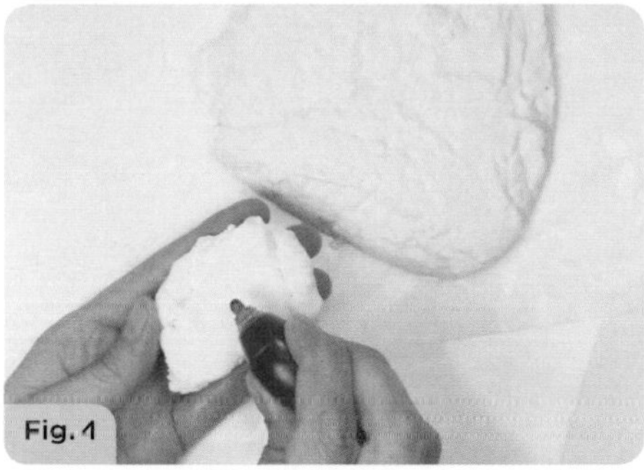

Fig. 4

Fig. 5

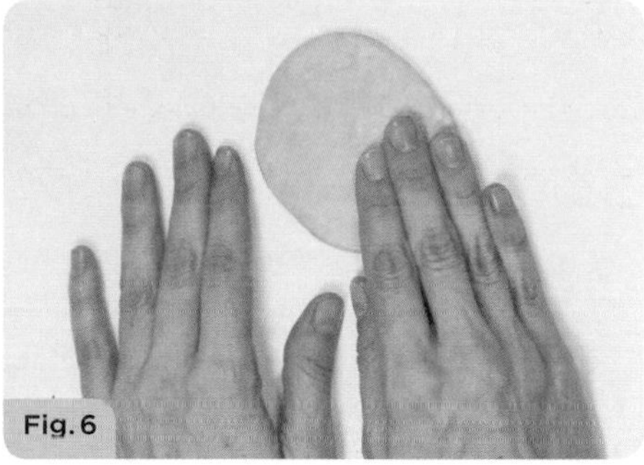

Fig. 6

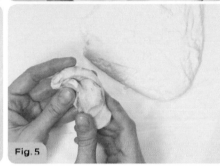
Fig. 7

2 Microwave on the defrost setting for two minutes. Use the spoon to stir. Continue to microwave until the candy has completely melted.

3 Mix in the corn syrup and stir until blended. (Fig. 2)

4 Pour the candy clay onto a strip of waxed paper. Allow it to cool and harden for a few hours or place it in the refrigerator for 30 minutes. (Fig. 3)

5 To add color to the clay, break off a piece and work it between your hands. It may be hard at first. Working with it for a couple of minutes will soften the clay.

6 Add one drop of food coloring in the center of the clay. Fold the clay inward toward the drop and work the color into the clay by kneading it. If you want

to prevent your hands from being stained, wear disposable gloves. (Fig. 4 & 5)

7 Place a sheet of wax paper on the table and sprinkle it with flour. Press the clay onto the wax paper. Use cookie cutters to cut out shapes or letters. (Fig. 6 & 7)

8 Use the candy clay to decorate sweet treats. Or place them in a cellophane bag with a bow and give them away as edible gifts!

RESOURCES

BOOKS FOR AIR-DRY CLAY CREATIONS

The following books were written for young artists to explore kiln-fired clay. However, the projects in these books can just as easily be created with air-dry clays.

Ceramics for Kids by Mary Ellis

The Great Clay Adventure by Ellen Kong

The Kids 'N' Clay Ceramics Book by Kevin Nierman and Elaine Arima

Exploring Clay with Children by Chris Utley and Mal Magson

Clay in the Primary School by Peter Clough

Super Simple Clay Projects by Karen Latchana Kenney

BOOKS FOR POLYMER CLAY CREATIONS

Kawaii Polymer Clay Creations by Emily Chen

The Polymer Clay Techniques Book by Sue Heaser

Modeling Clay Animals by Bernadette Cuxart

Modeling Clay Fantasy Characters by Bernadette Cuxart

Crazy Clay Creatures by Maureen Carlson

ONLINE RESOURCES

Here are some great online resources for the budding sculptor.

Clay Kids is a wonderful site with great Claymation videos as well as plenty of tips and tricks.

www.claykids.com

Crayola has a wide variety of kid friendly projects available on their website. Simply search clay to find an assortment of ideas to choose from.

www.crayola.com

ACKNOWLEDGMENTS

To the folks at Quarry books who helped hold this clueless girl's hand in the writing and photography of this book. I wouldn't have been able to do it without y'all.

To my husband, Mitch, for understanding my disappearing to the "clay room" each evening and weekend only to reappear with clay under my nails and stuck in my hair. Thank you for giving me the time and space to make big messes.

To my mom for her excellent cheerleading skills. You are always there to encourage me, and I love you for it.

To my sweet art teacherin' friends, who are always there to offer advice, encouragement, and hugs. The world is truly a better place with good friends.

And a big special thank you to my sweet students, who have taught me just as much about creativity, imagination, and mess making over the years as I've attempted to teach them. Teaching art is truly the best job there is, and I'm thrilled that I have the opportunity to do it!

ABOUT THE AUTHOR

Cassie Stephens has been teaching art to kindergarten through fourth grade students in the Nashville area for close to twenty years. Prior to art teaching, she was a terrible waitress, a miserable corn detasseler, and a lazy egg factory employee. A fateful voyage from the Midwest to the South, with her grandmother in tow, landed her an art educator position in Tennessee. She's been creating big messes with small people ever since.

If you ask Cassie's students what they love about art, you'll usually get one of two responses: "It's fun!" and "Because we play with clay!" Knowing just how much her students enjoy creating with clay, Cassie has introduced her students to a wide variety of projects, many of which you can find in the pages of this book. What she has discovered is that showing students ideas in working with clay is fun, but the real magic is in seeing just

where her students will take these ideas and what they will create.

When not elbows deep in mess making merriment, you can find Cassie blogging all about her adventures in art education at cassiestephens.blogspot.com.

INDEX